Flowers and Whimsy

Adult Coloring Book of
Fun to Color Ornamental Floral Patterns,
Whimsical Butterflies, Dragonflies and More!

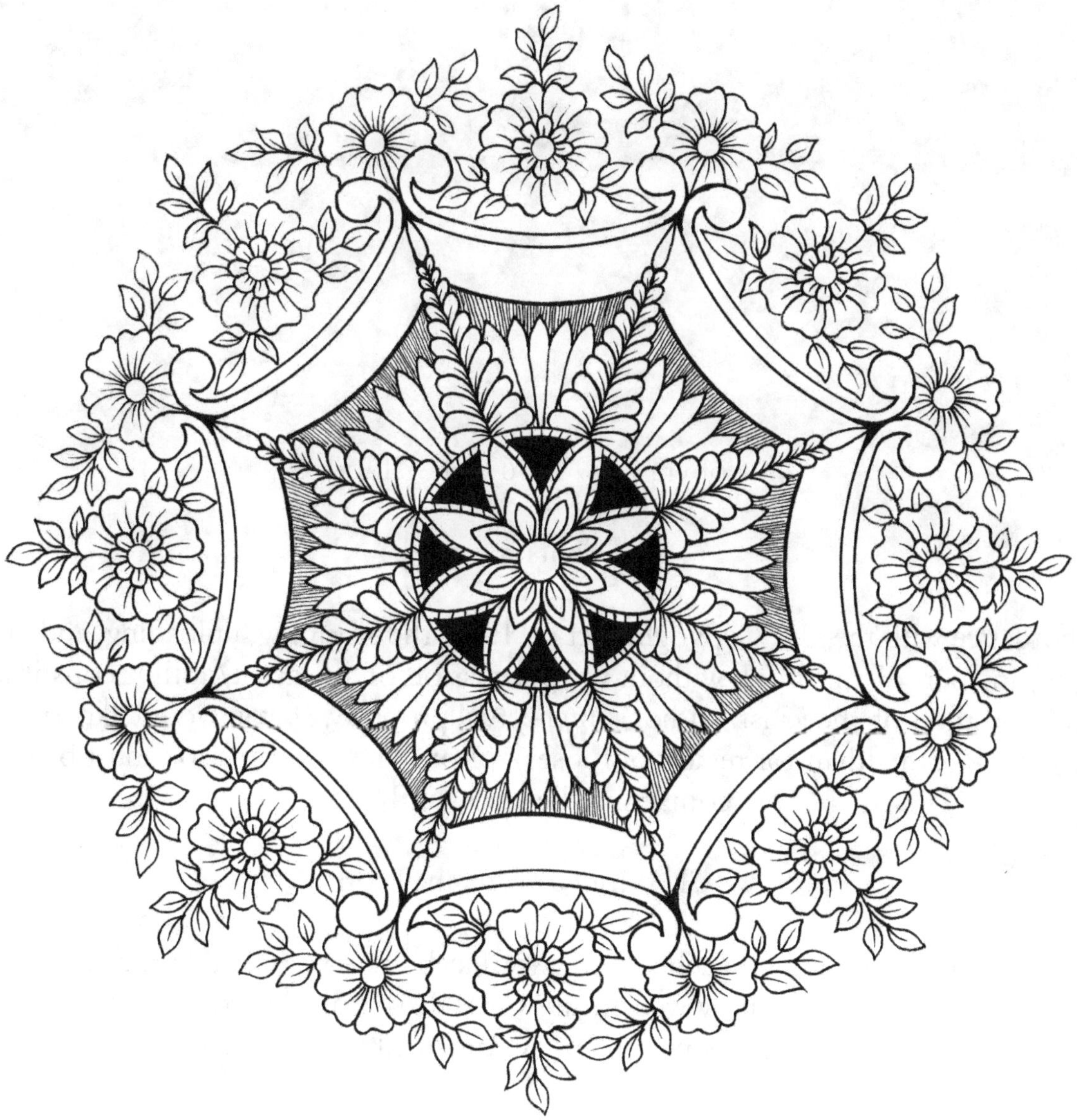

Illustrations by: C. L. Aldridge

ISBN-13: 978-1540731814
ISBN-10: 1540731812

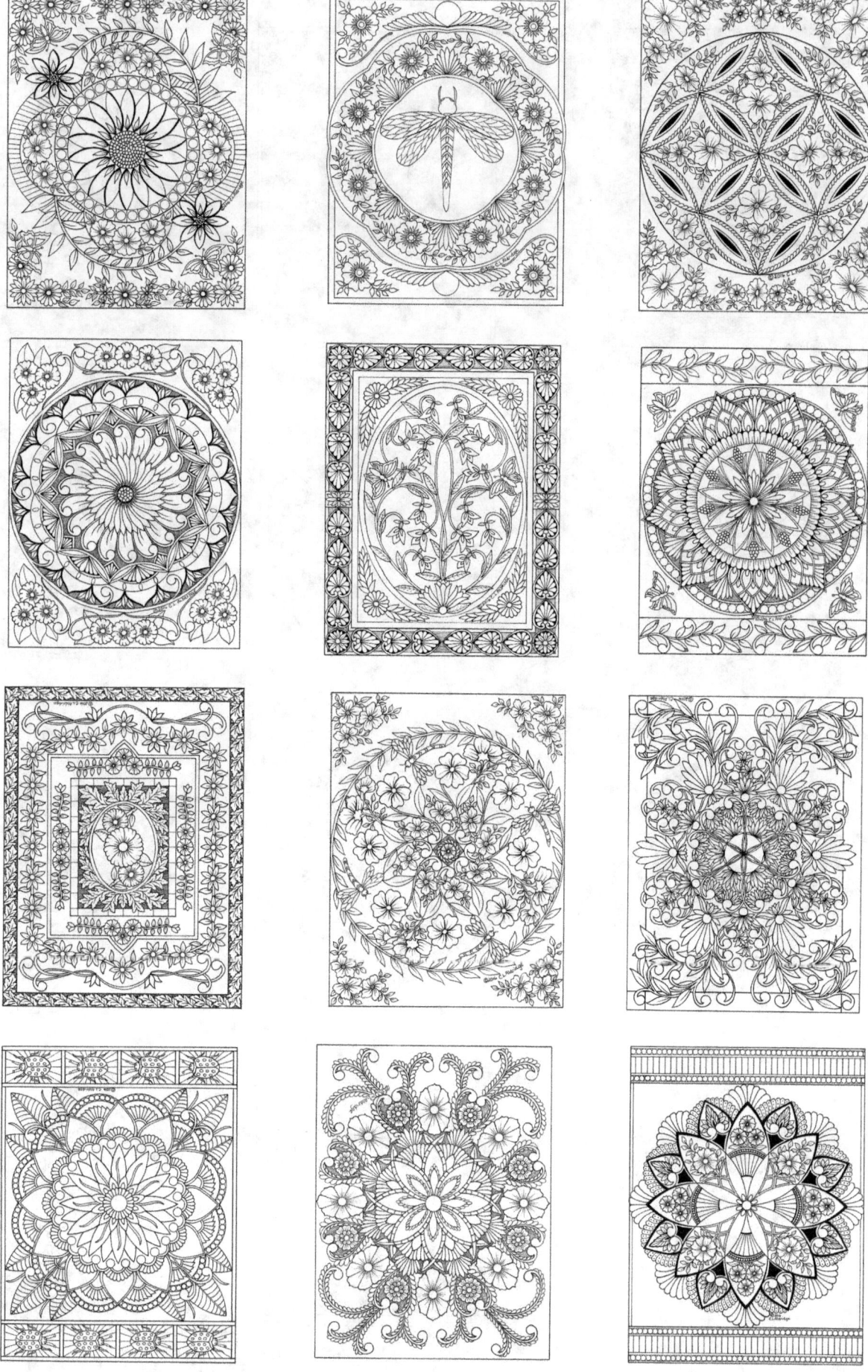

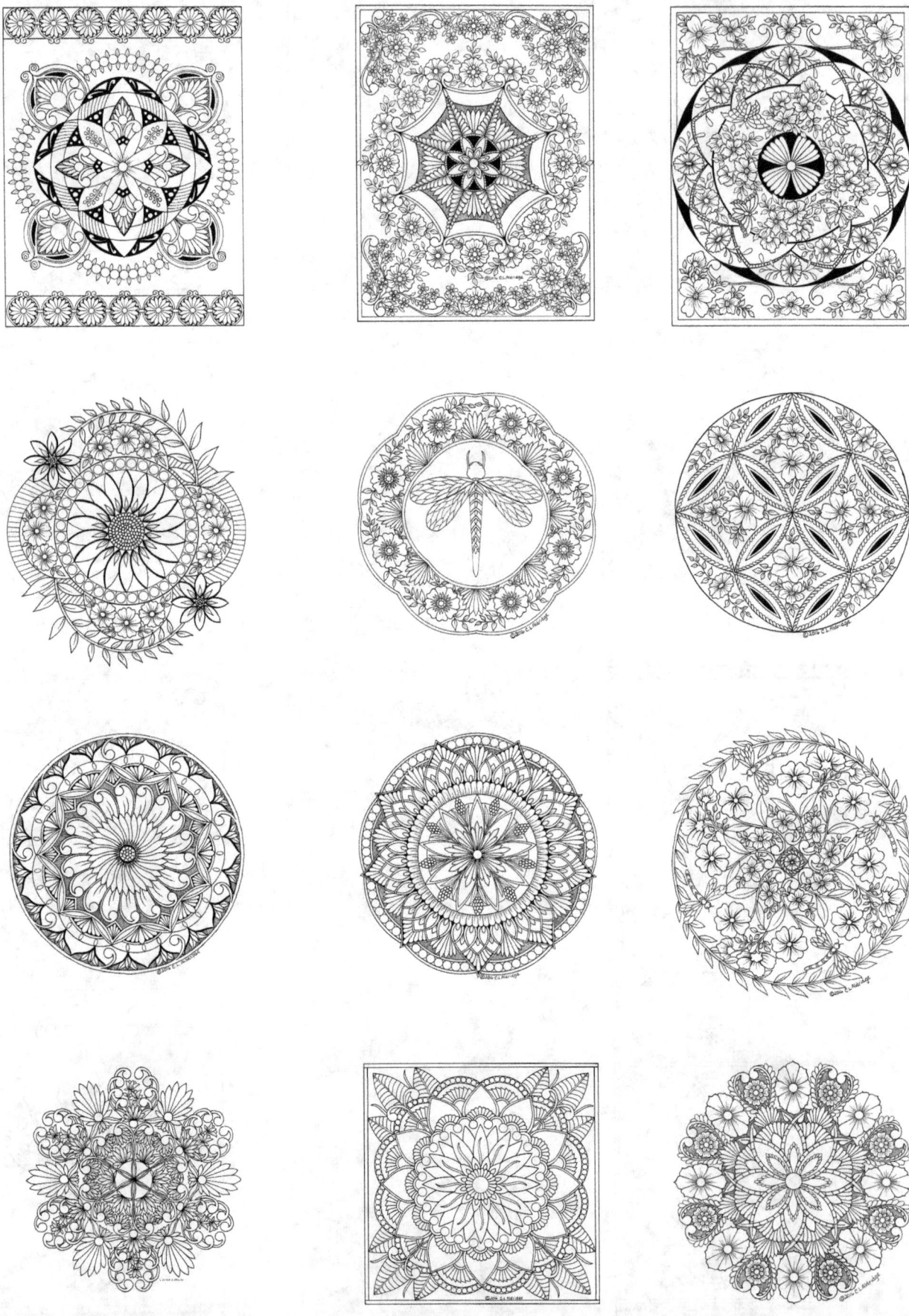

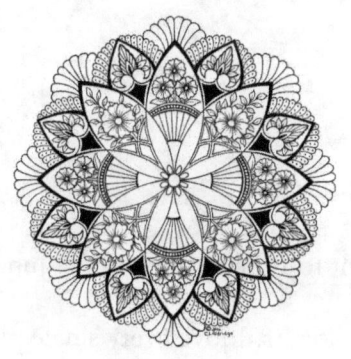
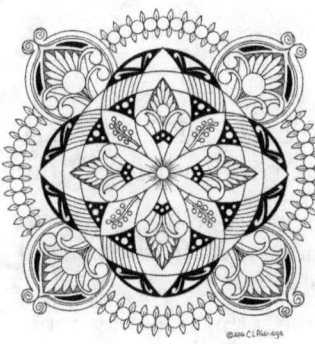
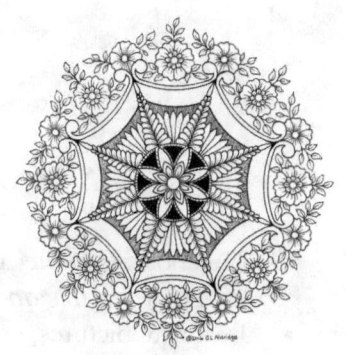

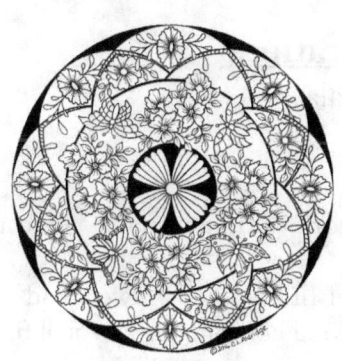

PLUS 6 BONUS DRAWINGS -
For the first time in a print book,
these six drawings have previously
only been offered in the Artists
Etsy shop at :
www.Etsy.com/shop/CLAldridgeArt

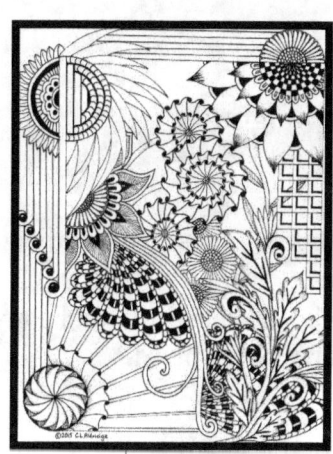
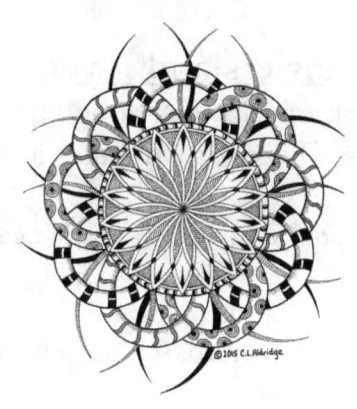
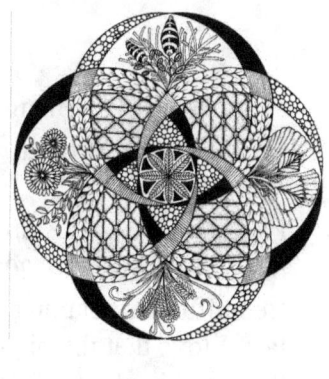

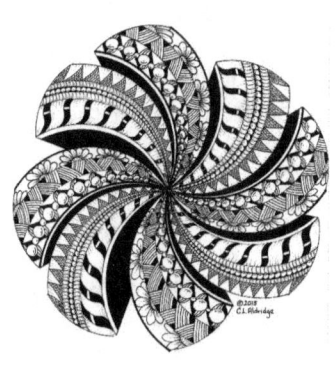
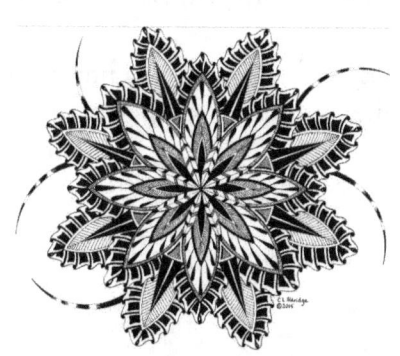
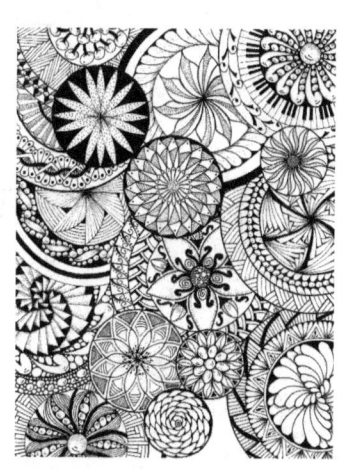

Also by C. L. Aldridge

Flowers and Dreams
A Coloring Book of Beautiful Botanical Symmetry

- This book is so elegant that when you finish coloring it you want to frame every one! - Jun. 16, 2016 ~ *Amazon Customer*
- Beautiful pictures, expertly drawn... this book is a must for all colorists. I love every single picture in this book - May 6, 2016 ~ *Patti*

Adult Coloring Book of Flower Inspirations
Beautiful Floral Patterns, Botanical Mandalas, Gemstones, Lovely Words and More!

- I love this artist and this book has everything I love about her work, and then some! You can't go wrong with Flower Inspirations! - June 7, 2016 ~ *Teresa Z*
- C. L. Aldridge has hit it out of the ballpark again! Just as with her first book, "Flowers and Dreams," this one is filled with the most unique and gorgeous floral coloring pages you'll find. Her pages are designed with consideration for any medium you choose to use. I'll be anxiously awaiting the release of a third book! - June 10, 2016 ~ *E. Siegel*

Flowers and Flyers
Adult Coloring Book of Flowers, Songbirds, Hummingbirds, Butterflies, Owls, Ornamentals and More!

- I have all 3 of C L Aldridge's books. I own lots of adult coloring books. These 3 are at the top of my list! - Sept. 30, 2016 ~ *C. Ames*
- Beautiful and relaxing to color! This is my first C. L. Aldridge book, but it will not be my last. I love that the pictures are one-sided, so I don't have to worry about bleed-through. Sept. 30, 2016 ~ *L. Mason*

Travel Size Book of Flowers, Birds Butterflies and More!
Your Coloring Book for the Road.

- Measures 6" x 9", just the right size to tuck in a purse, a travel bag or a desk drawer.
- 36 (12 from each of the larger books above) perfectly sized 5" x 7" illustrations for the busy colorist on the run.
- Easy to remove pages to mount on greeting cards, in frames or just satisfy the creative urge to color something beautiful.
- Single-Sided pages. 60 lb medium weight paper.

For all the colorists across the world that have encouraged me to keep drawing each and every day; and upon learning of a book featuring not only my signature full page illustrations, but single Mandalas too, urged me to please hurry. This one is for you! I hope you enjoy it as much as I enjoyed drawing it for you.

A very special thank you to colorists: Virginia Sanders Cole, Susan Curry, Shirley Olson and Jill Fanning for so generously allowing me to use their colored renderings of my drawings on the cover of this book.

* * * * *

<u>IMPORTANT INFORMATION FOR USING THIS BOOK</u>

- This book contains 48 hand-drawn illustrations to color, each is printed SINGLE SIDED (back is blank). 15 whole page designs, 13 Mandala only designs, plus two types of bonus pages!

- Many illustrations are printed in TWO SIZES, a full size page and a crafters size (suitable for a 5" x 7" frame, mounting to a greeting card face or scrapbook page, etc). Please note the crafters sizes are also single sided and are printed two on a page.

- The pages are printed on #60 lb bright white paper which performs well for all brands of colored pencils and crayons, without the need of a blotter page.

- To avoid any "Uh Oh's" and the associated disappointment, **Marker and Gel Pen users are STRONGLY ENCOURAGED to USE A BLOTTER SHEET** behind the drawing to avoid any possibility of bleed through to the next page. Several blank blotter and color testing pages are provided at the end of this book.

- Most IMPORTANT of all: Relax, have fun, stand-up and stretch often, and remember that sometimes the most beautiful things come from what we think at first are mistakes, but which turn out to be art's way of working magic!

This Book
Belongs To:

_____

_____

©2016 C.l.Aldridge

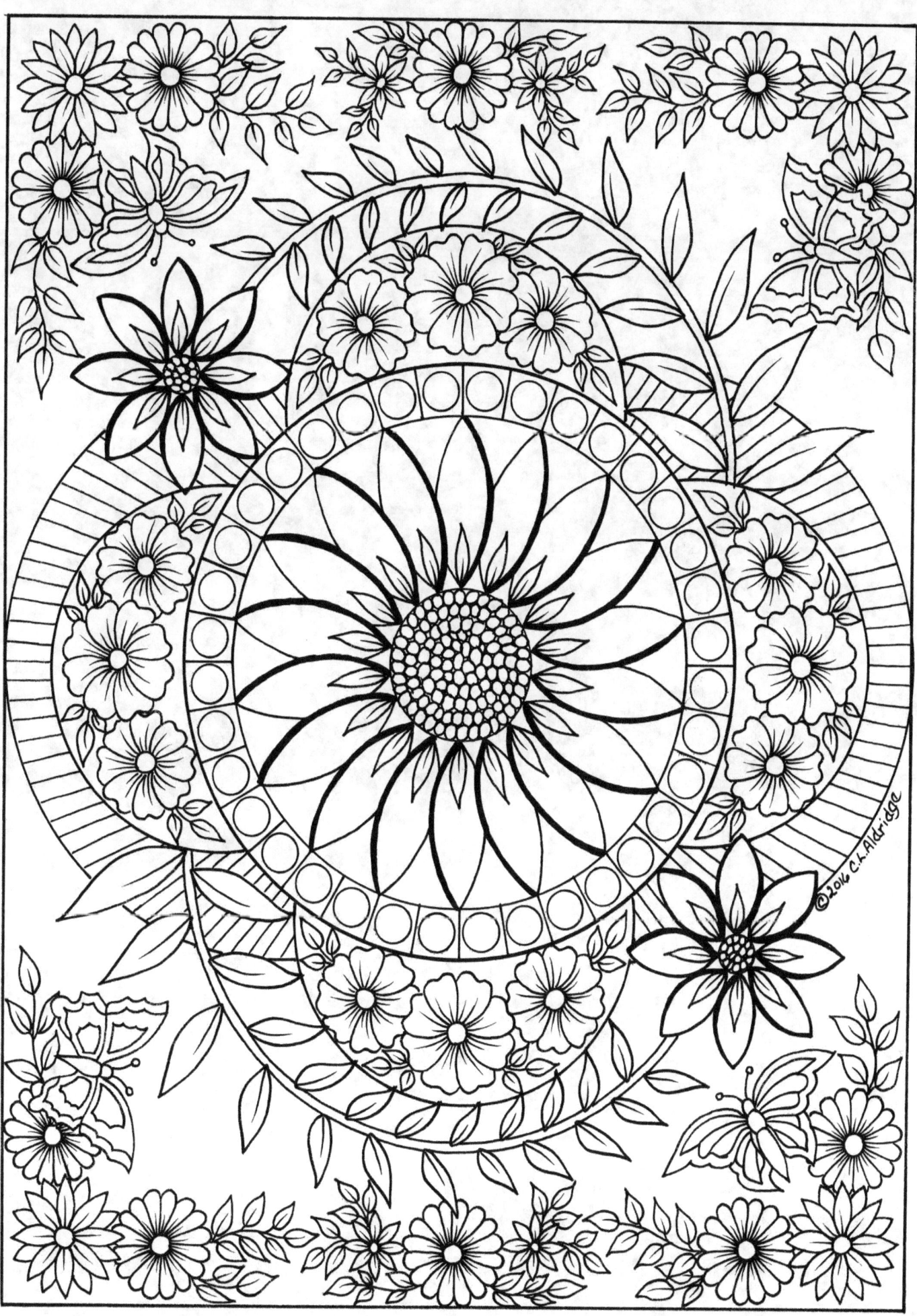

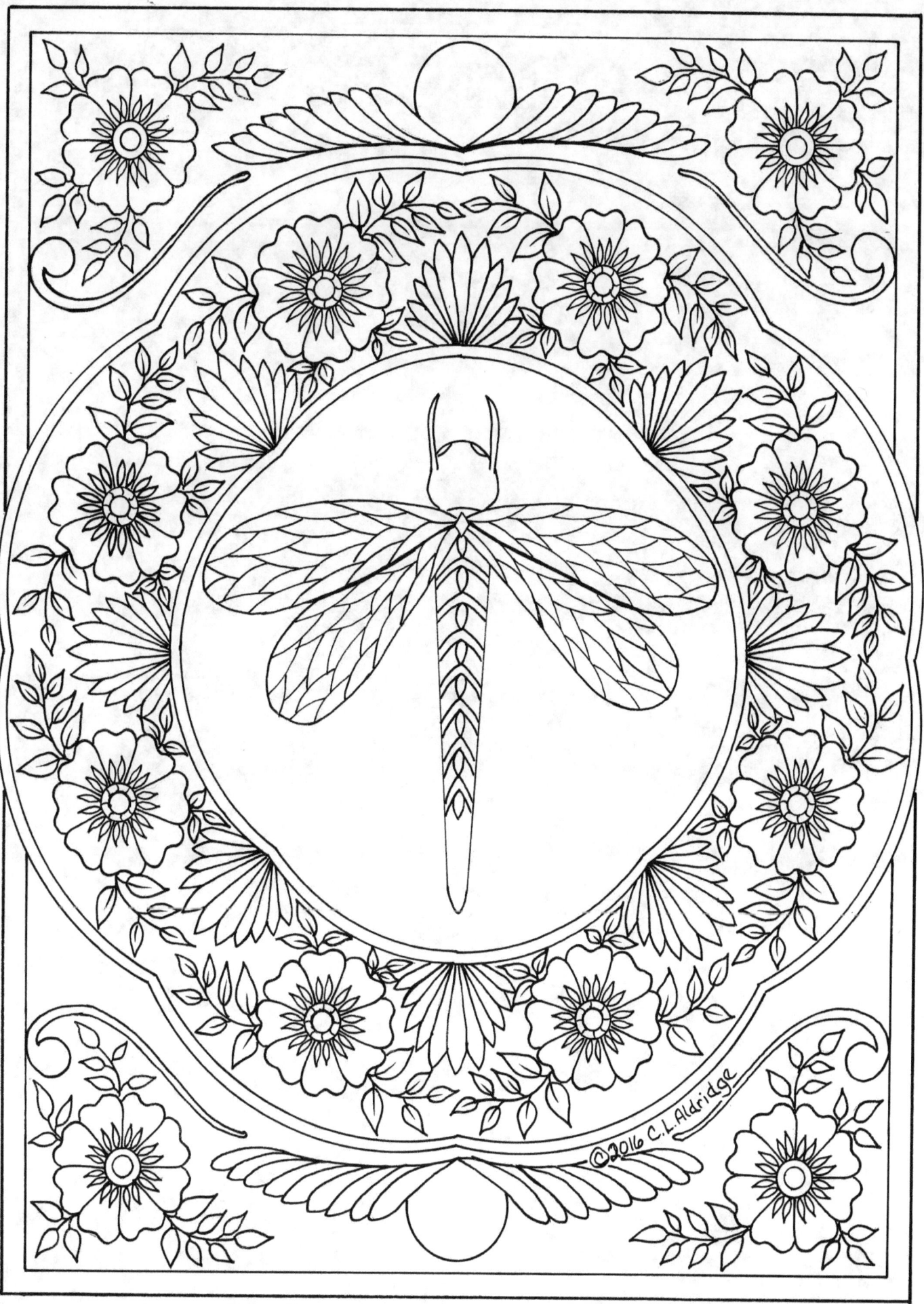
©2016 C.L. Aldridge

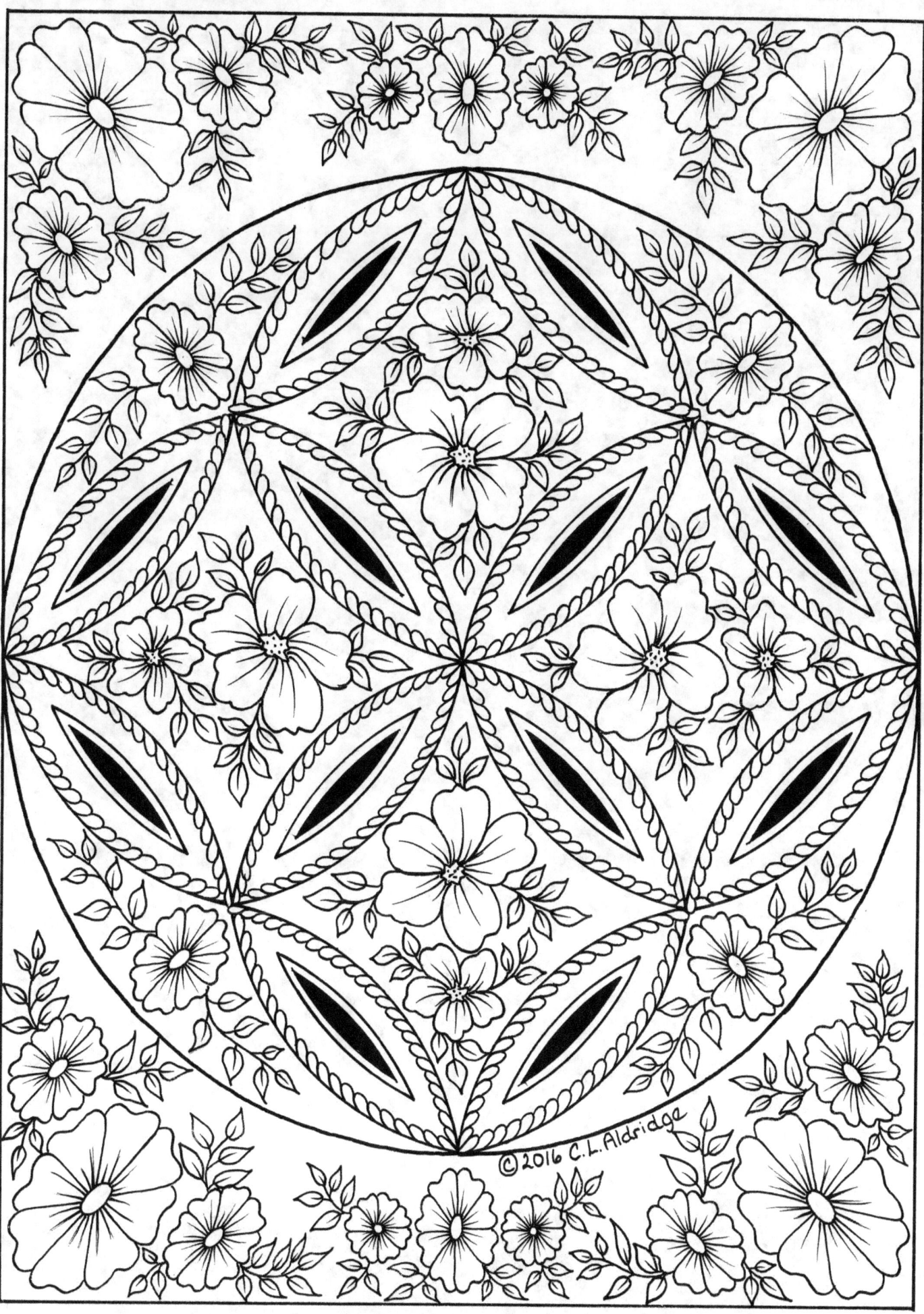

© 2016 C.L. Aldridge

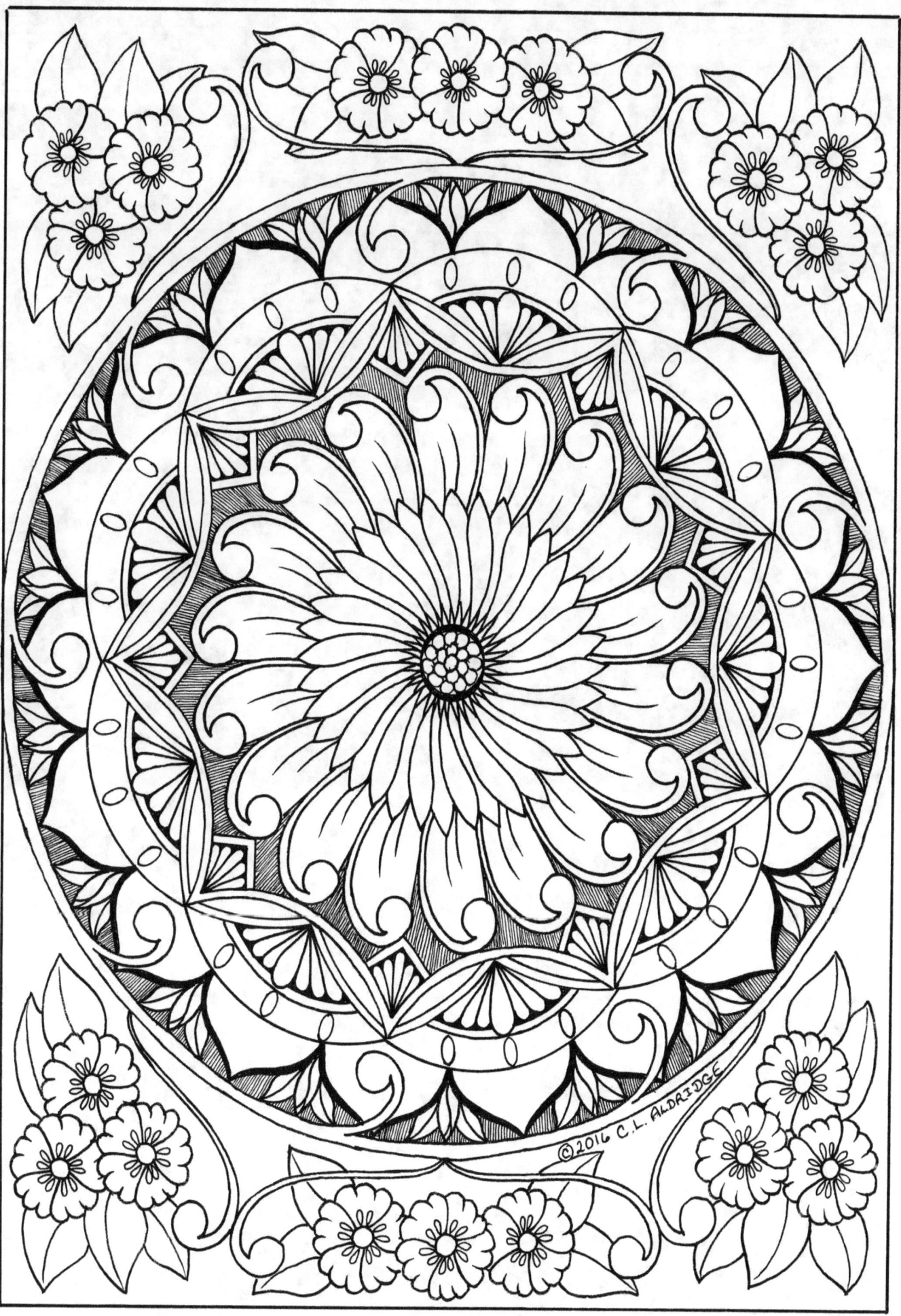
©2016 C.L. ALDRIDGE

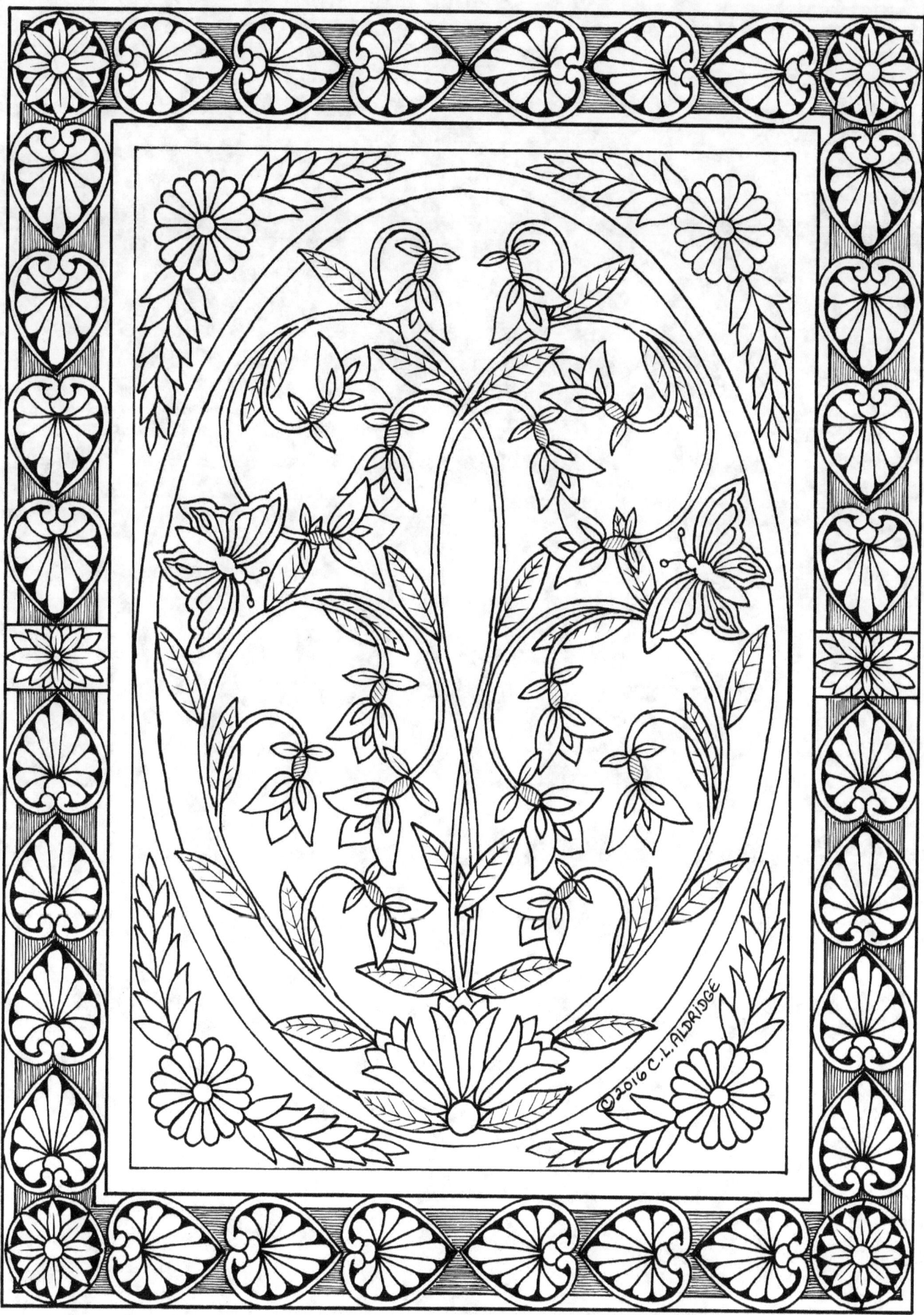

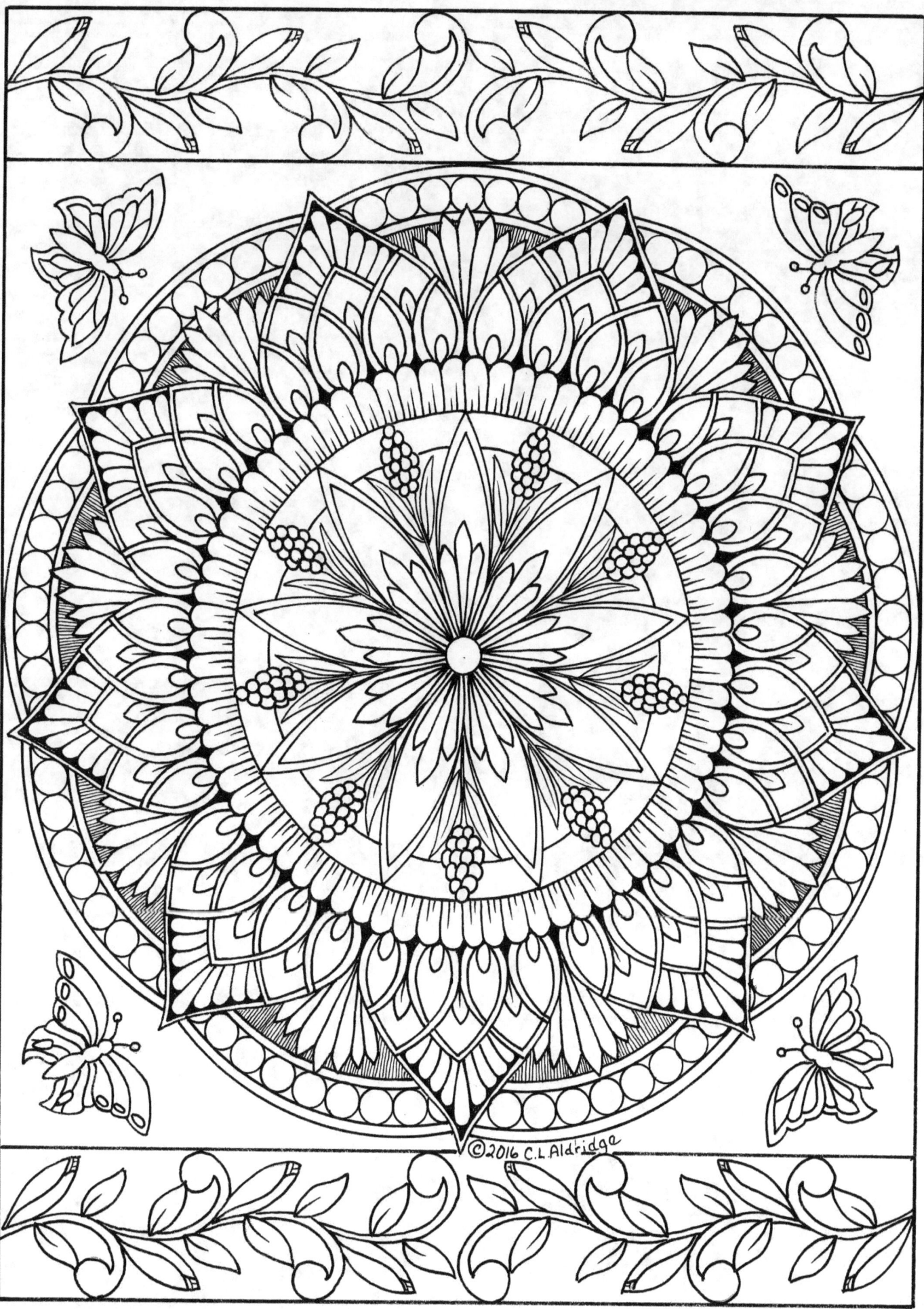

©2016 C.L.Aldridge

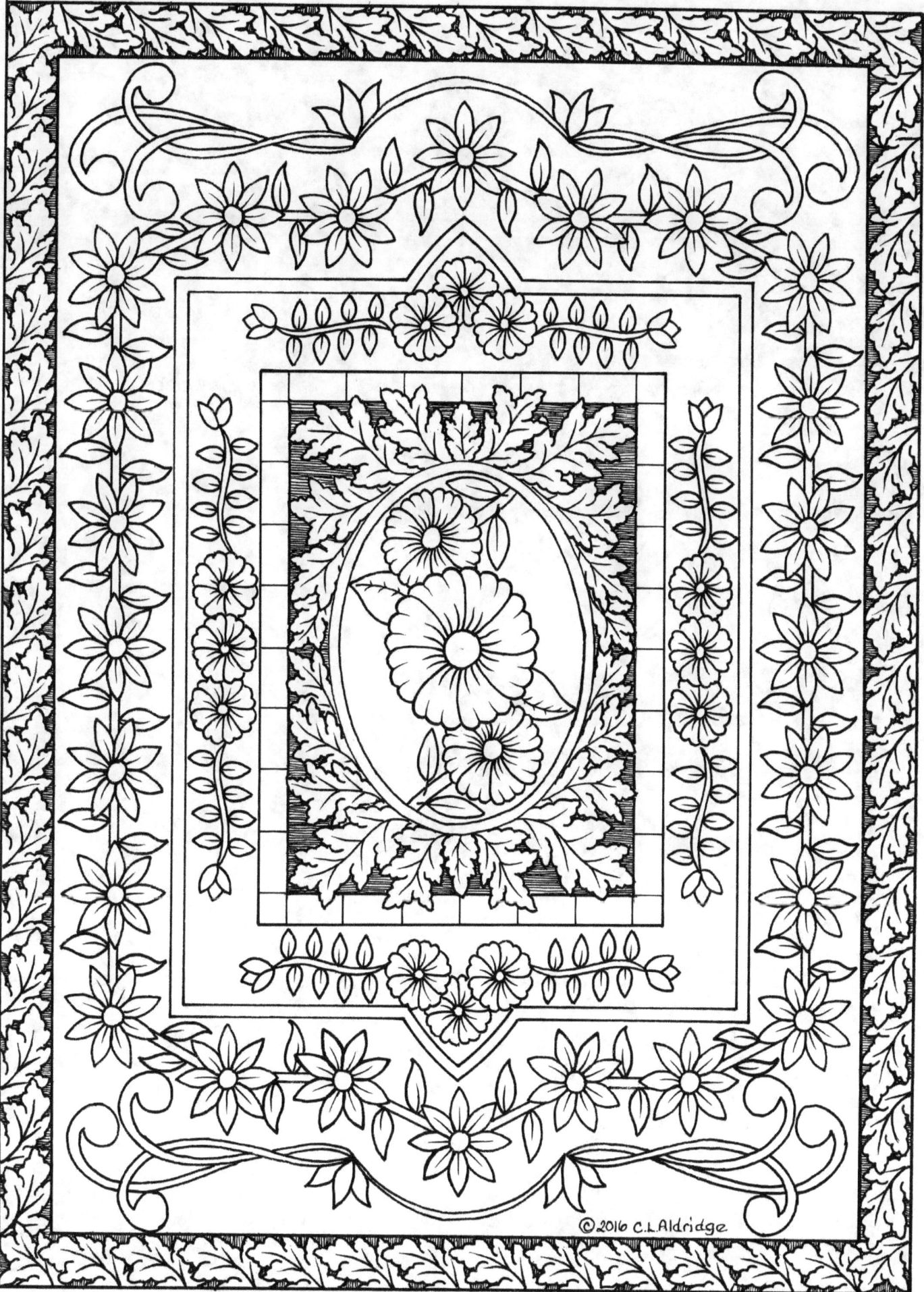

©2016 C.L.Aldridge

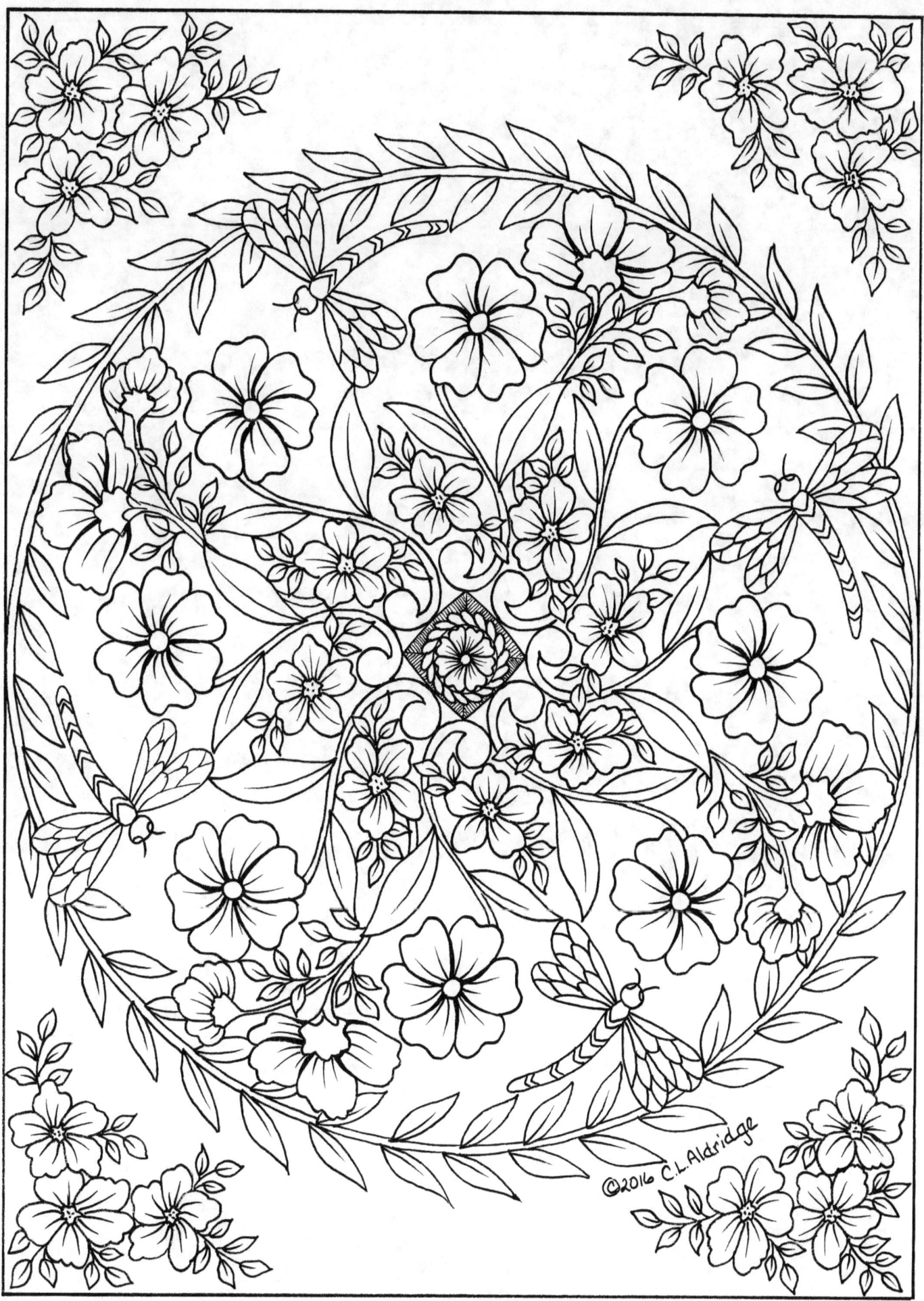
©2016 C.L. Aldridge

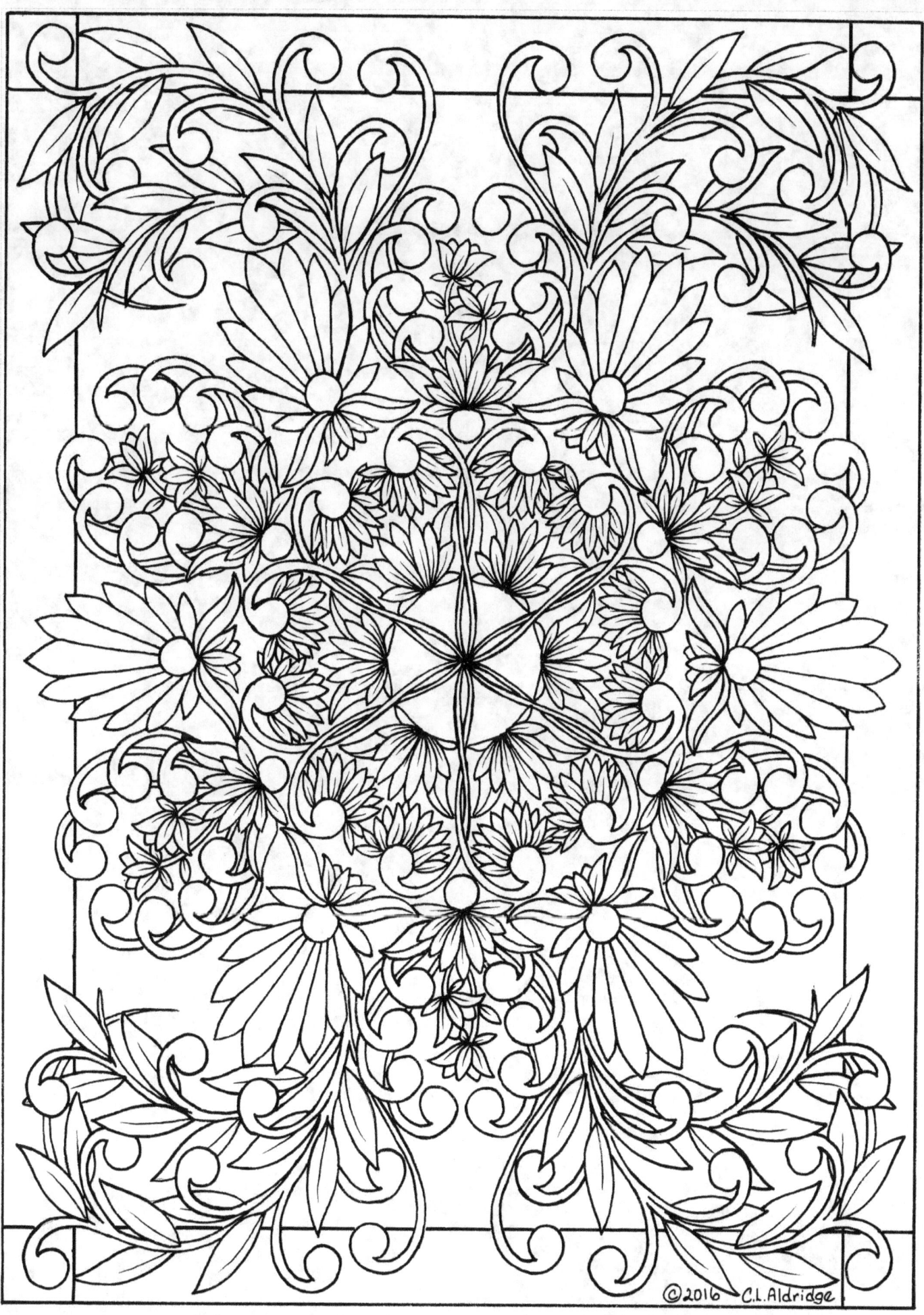

©2016 C.L.Aldridge

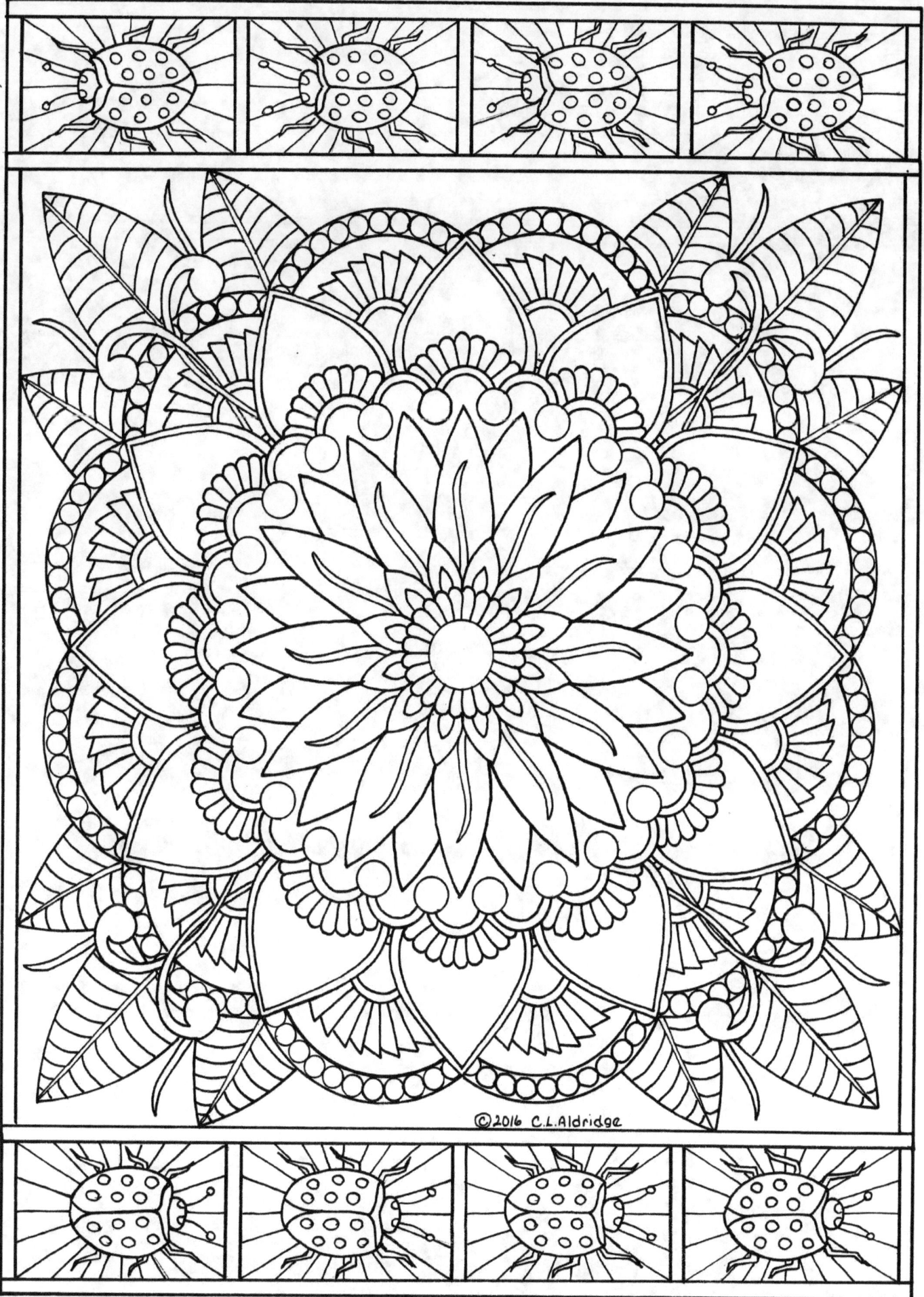

©2016 C.L.Aldridge

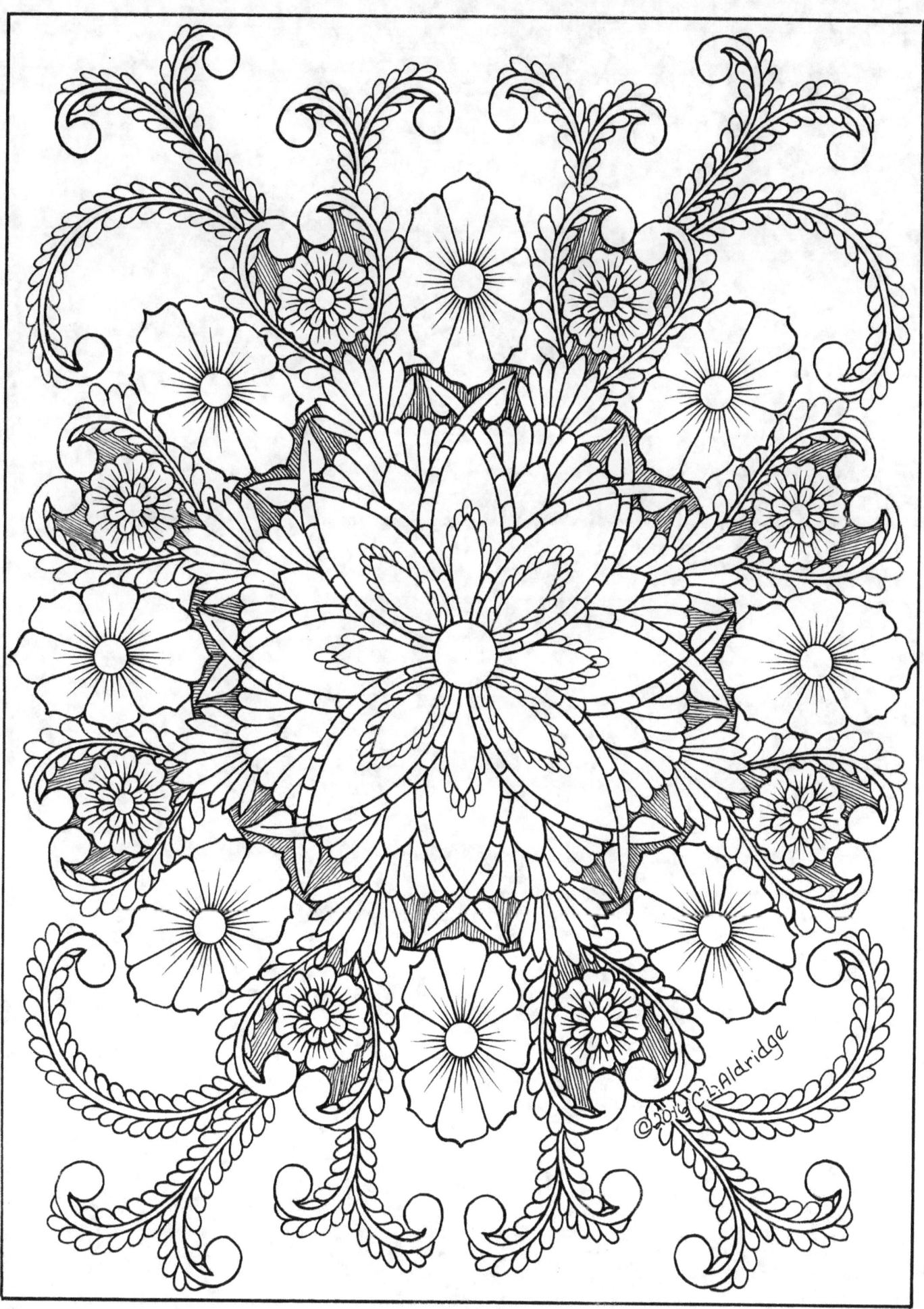

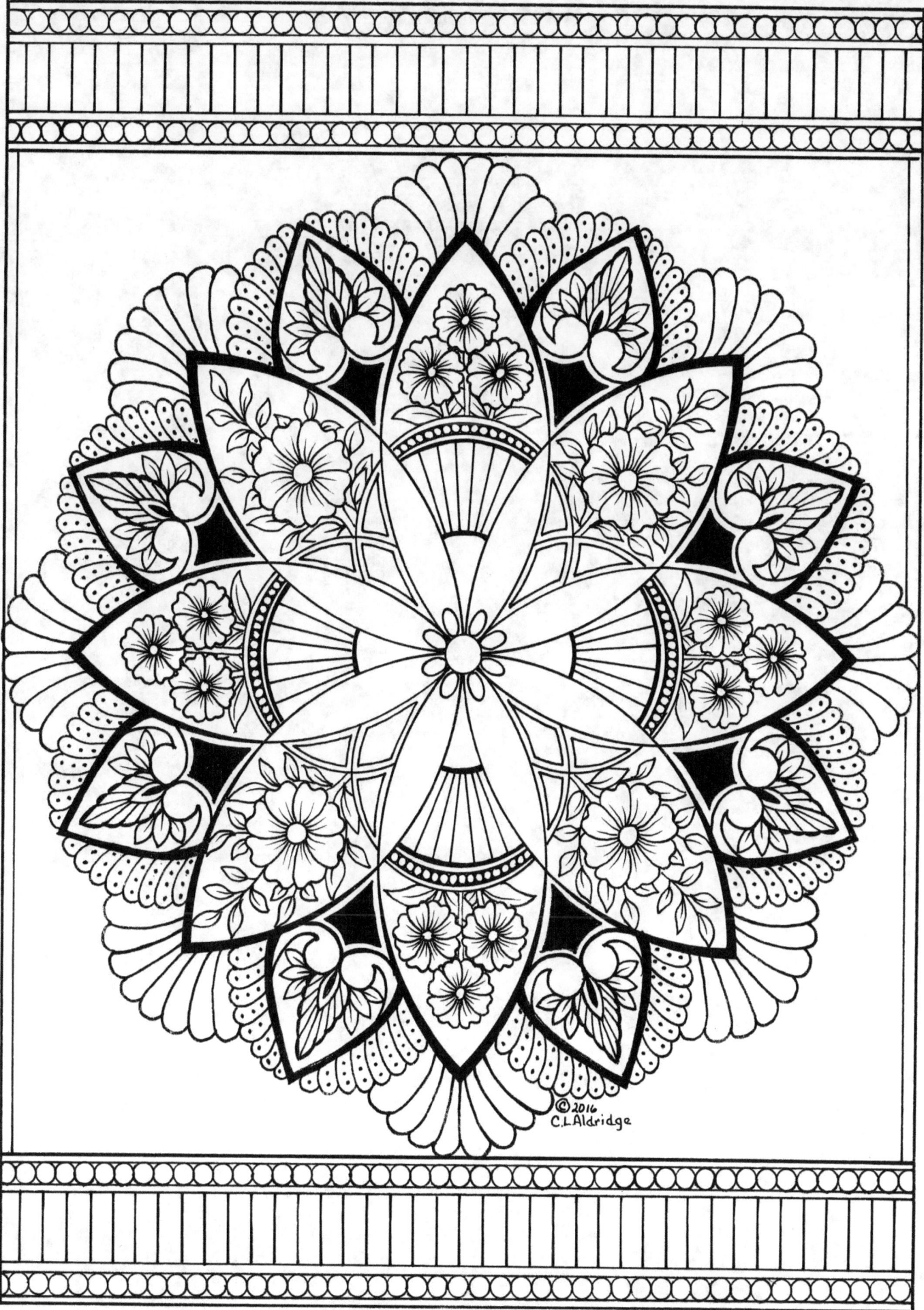
© 2016
C.L.Aldridge

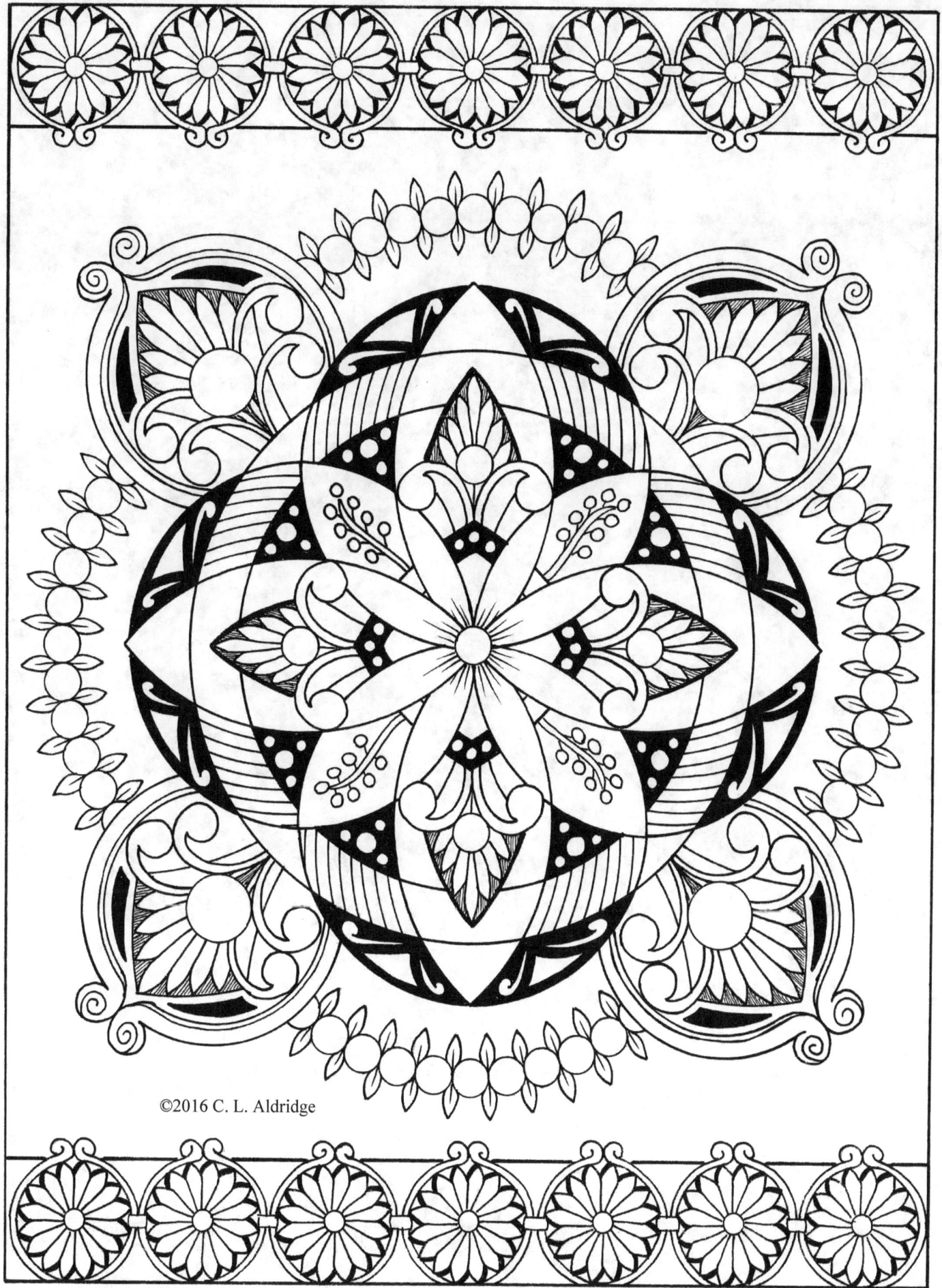

©2016 C. L. Aldridge

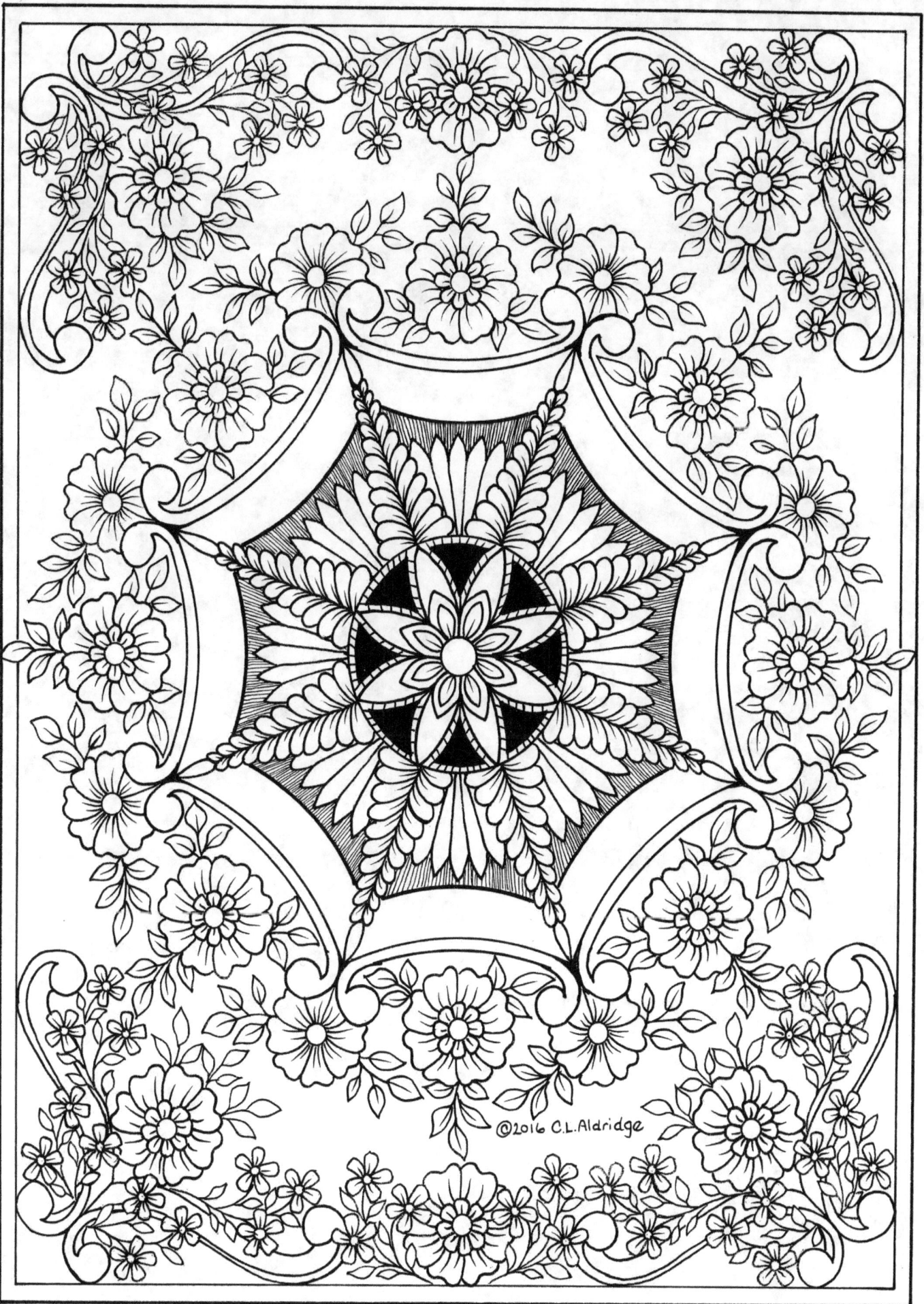
©2016 C.L.Aldridge

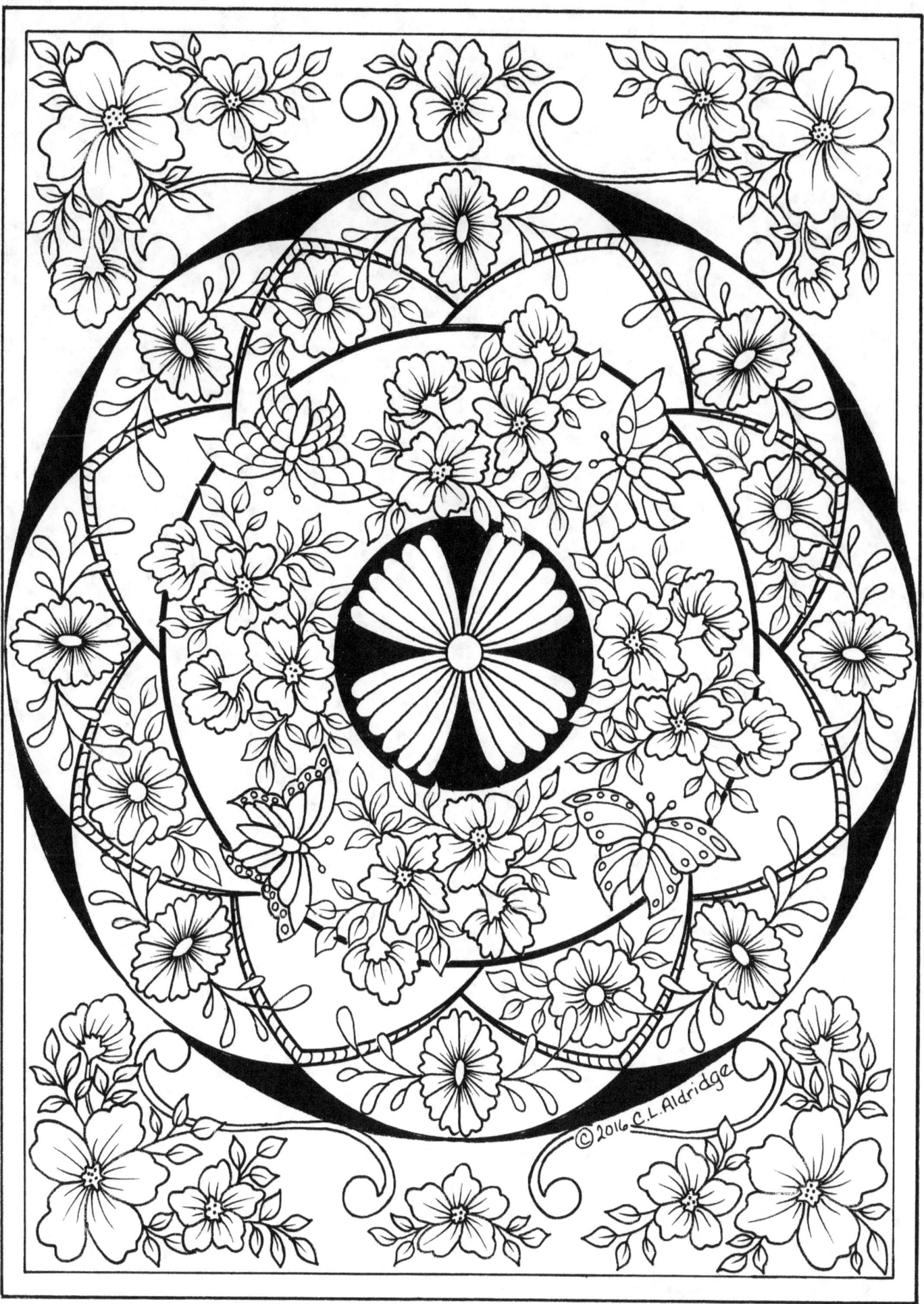
© 2016 C.L. Aldridge

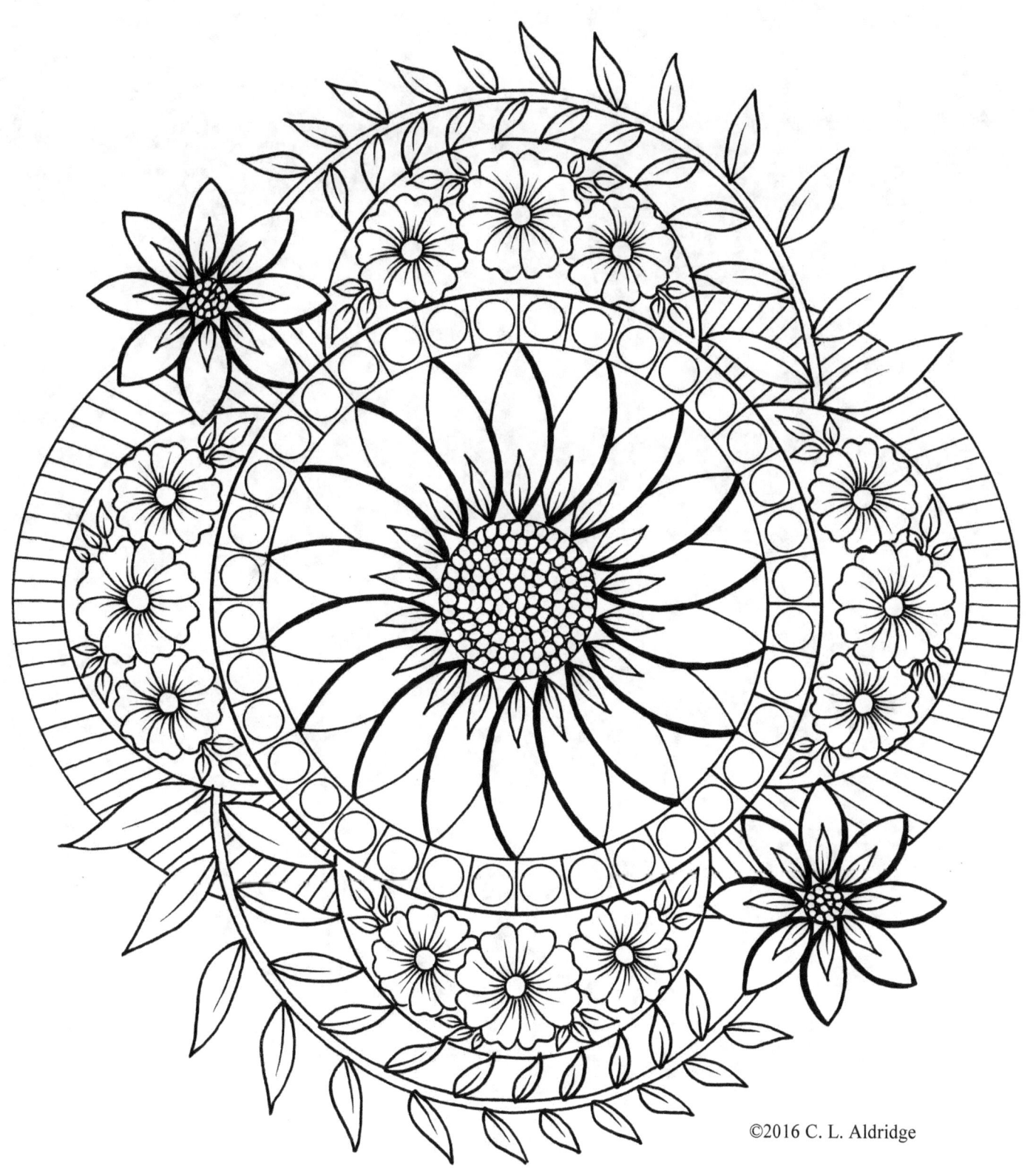

©2016 C. L. Aldridge

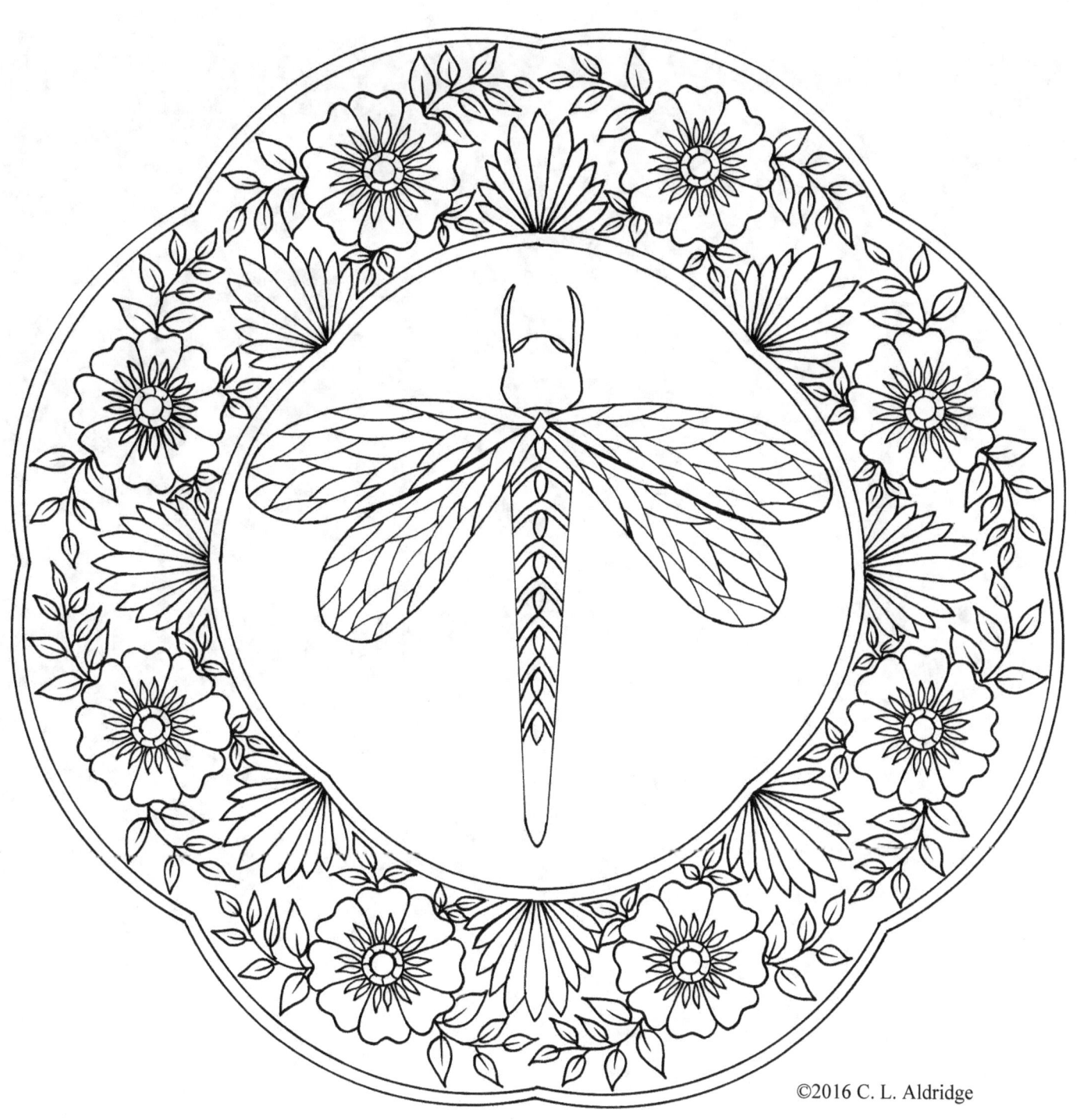

©2016 C. L. Aldridge

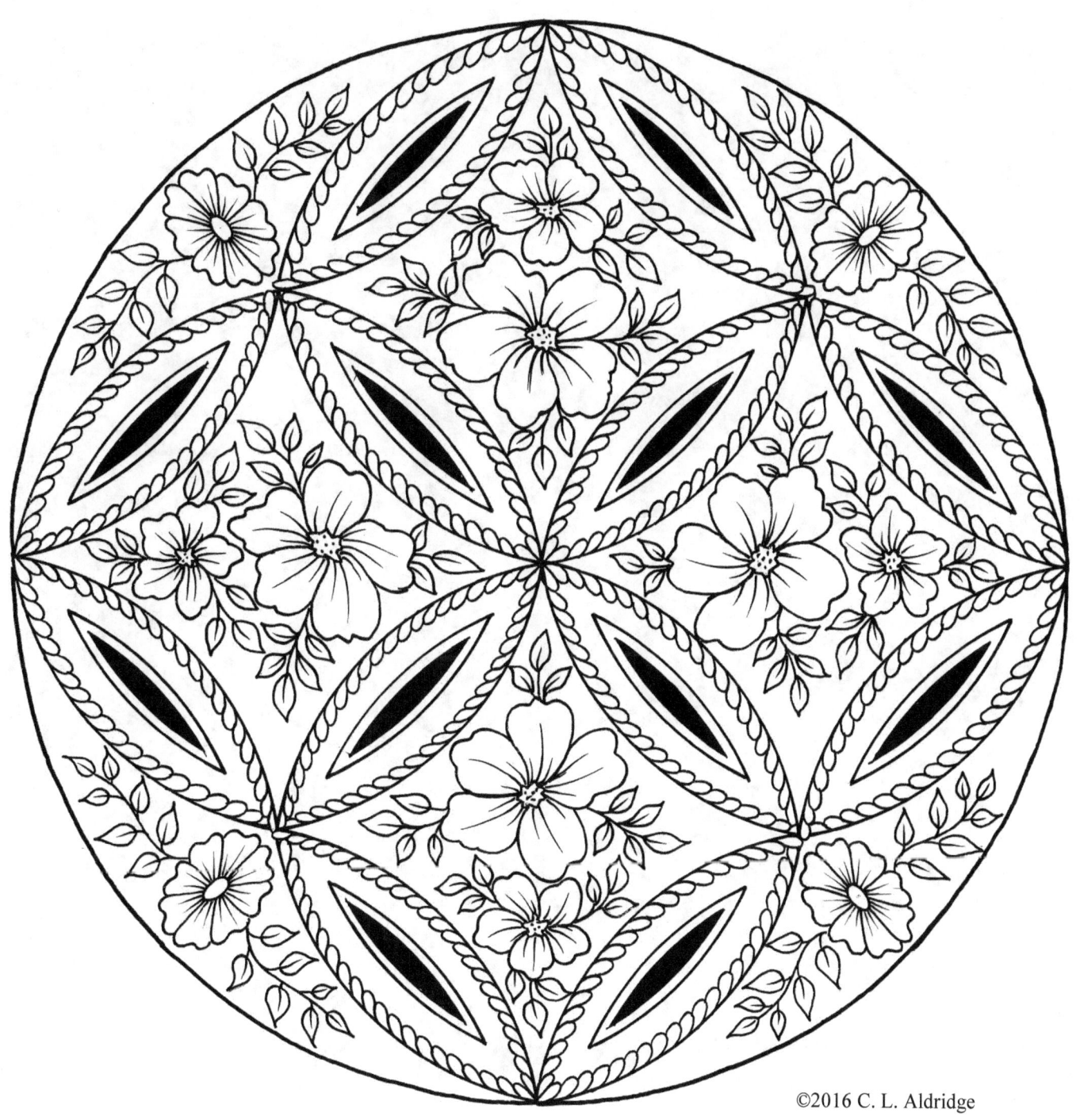

©2016 C. L. Aldridge

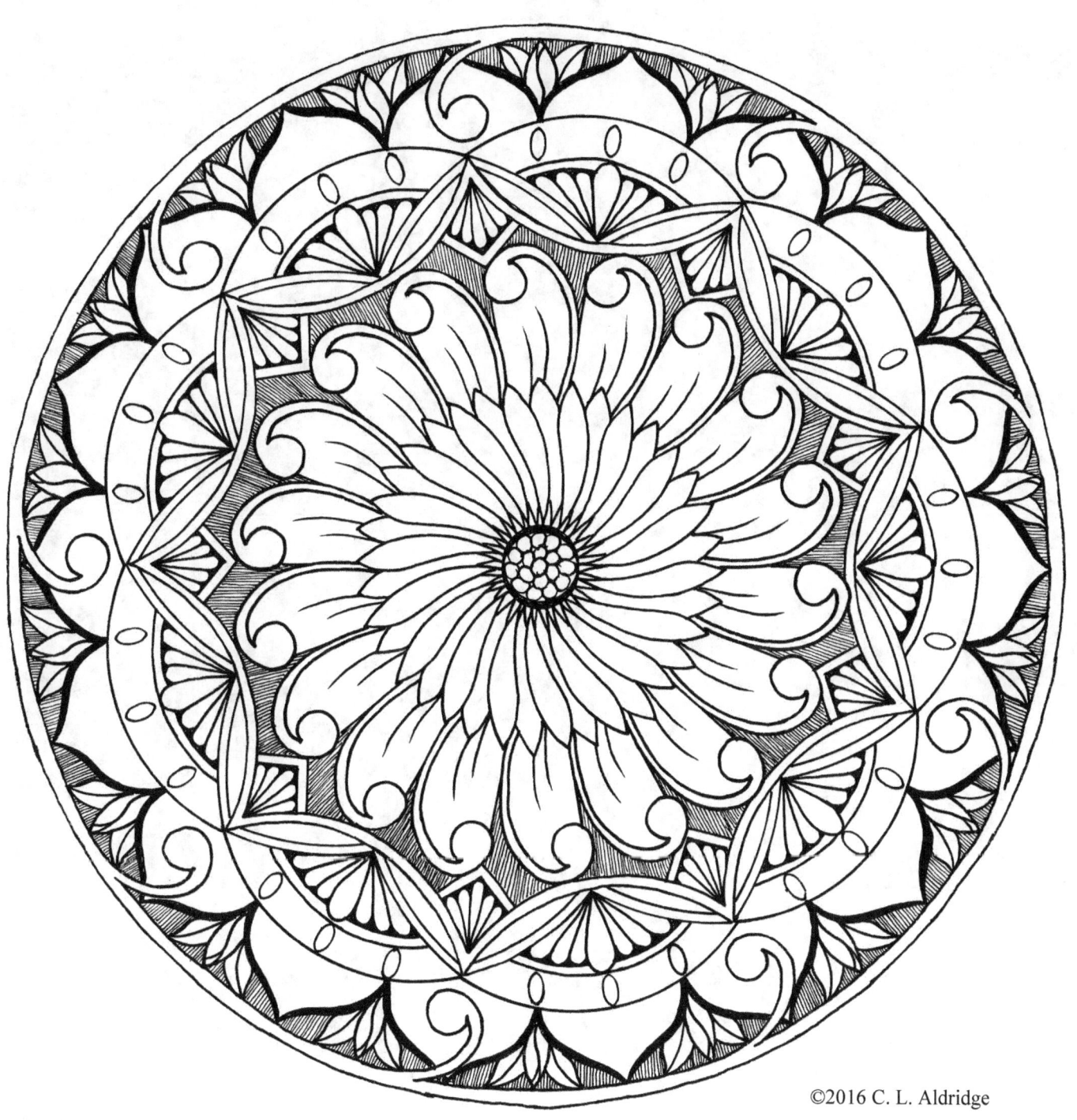

©2016 C. L. Aldridge

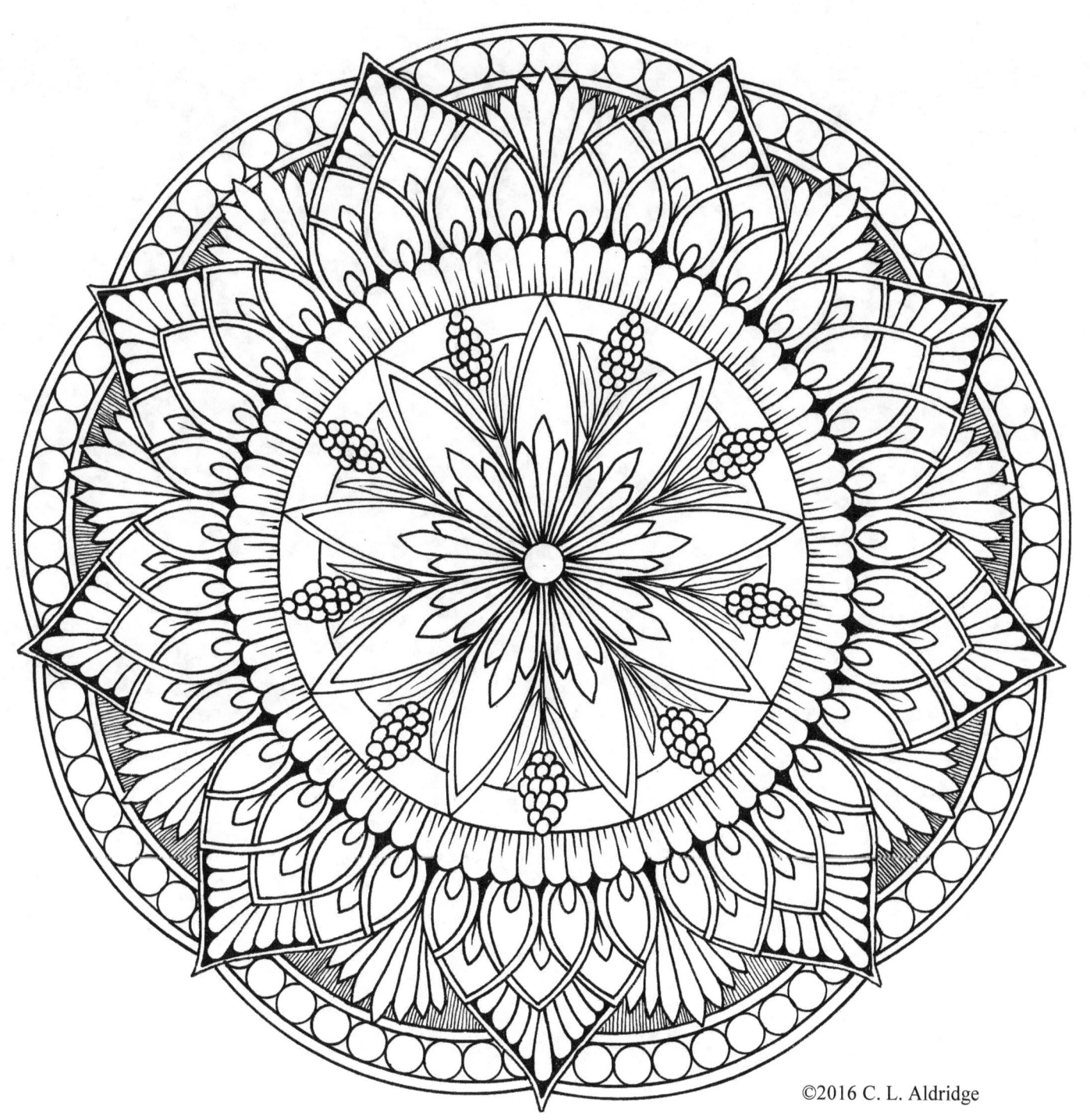

©2016 C. L. Aldridge

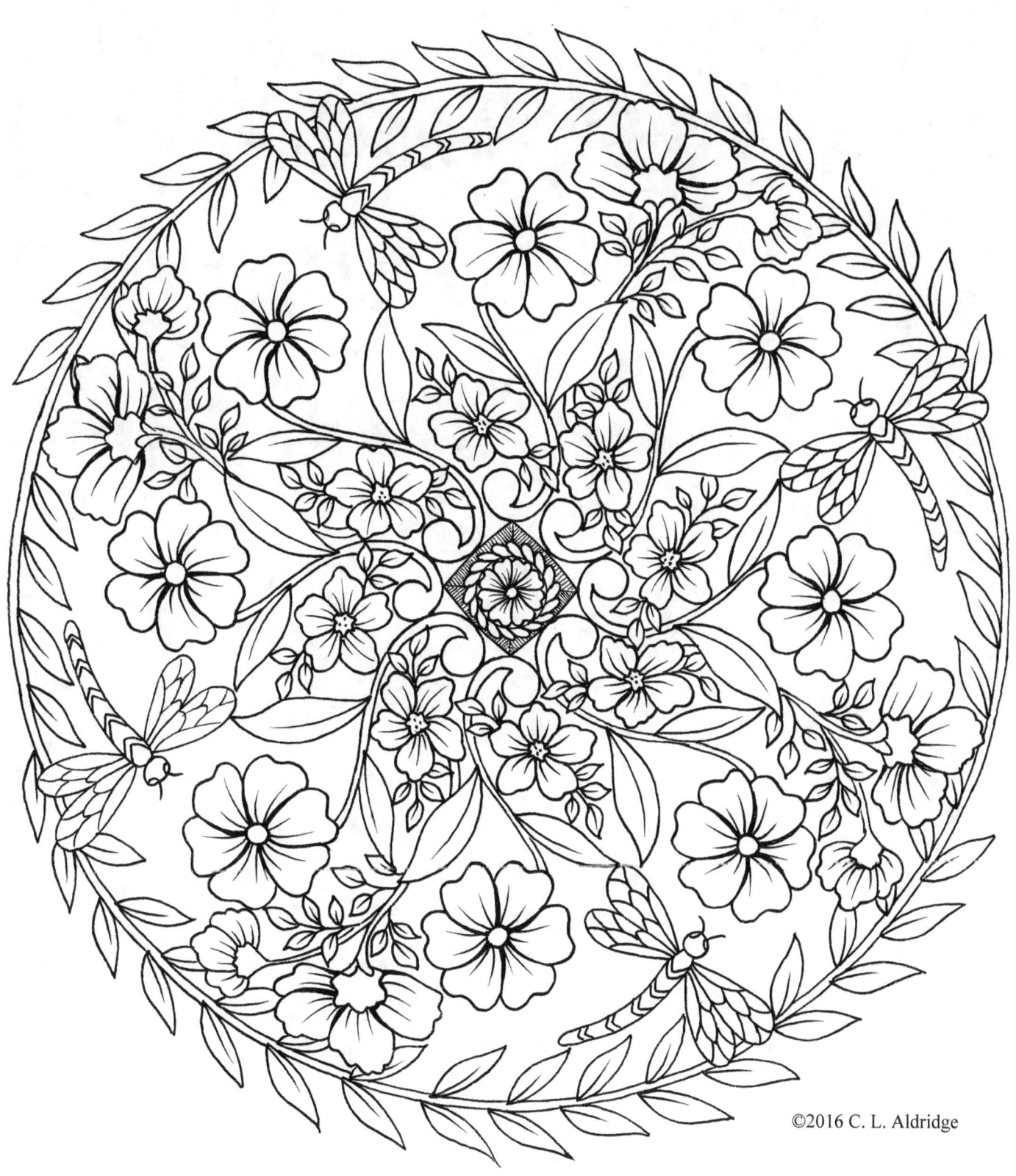

©2016 C. L. Aldridge

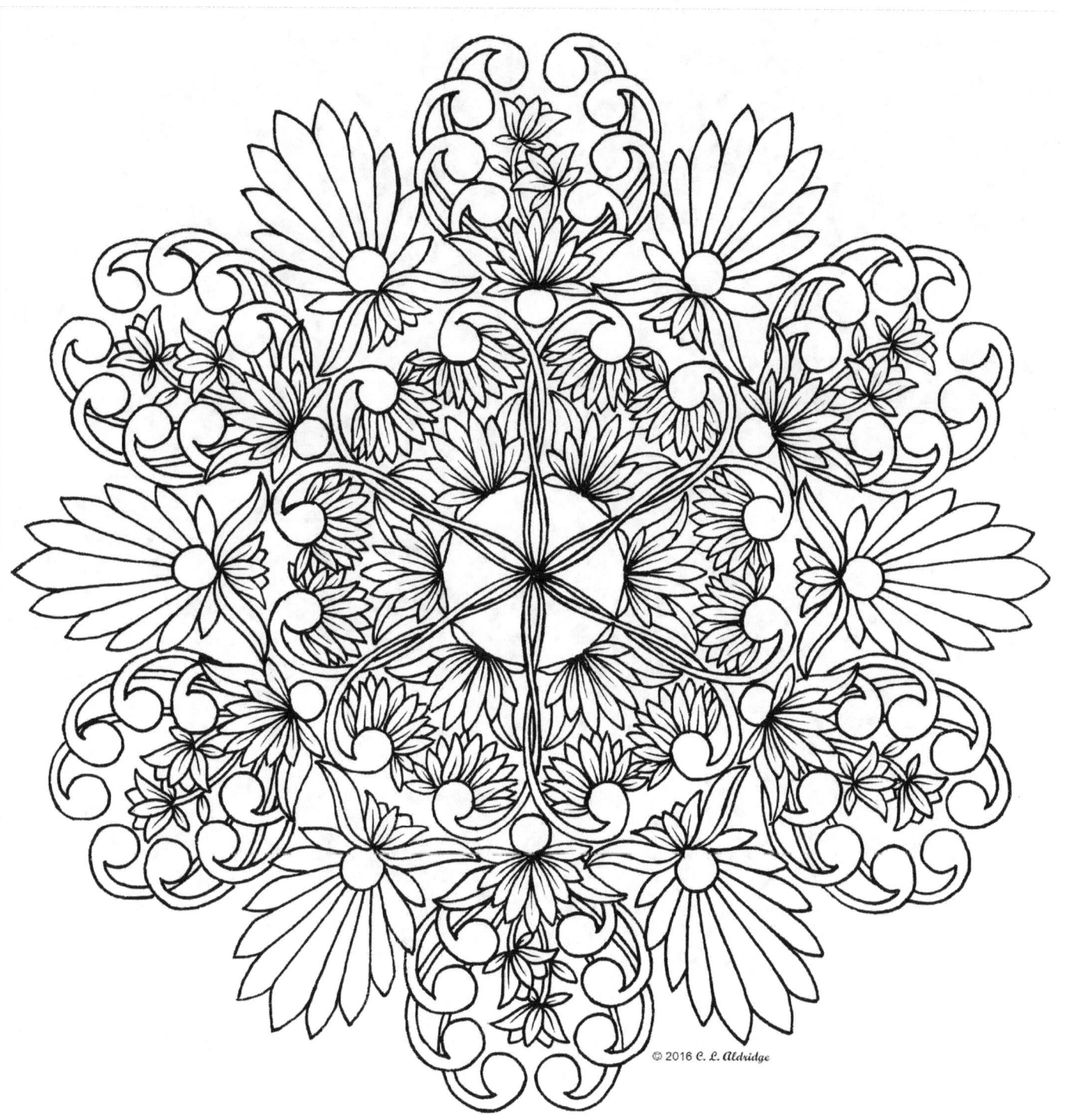
© 2016 C. L. Aldridge

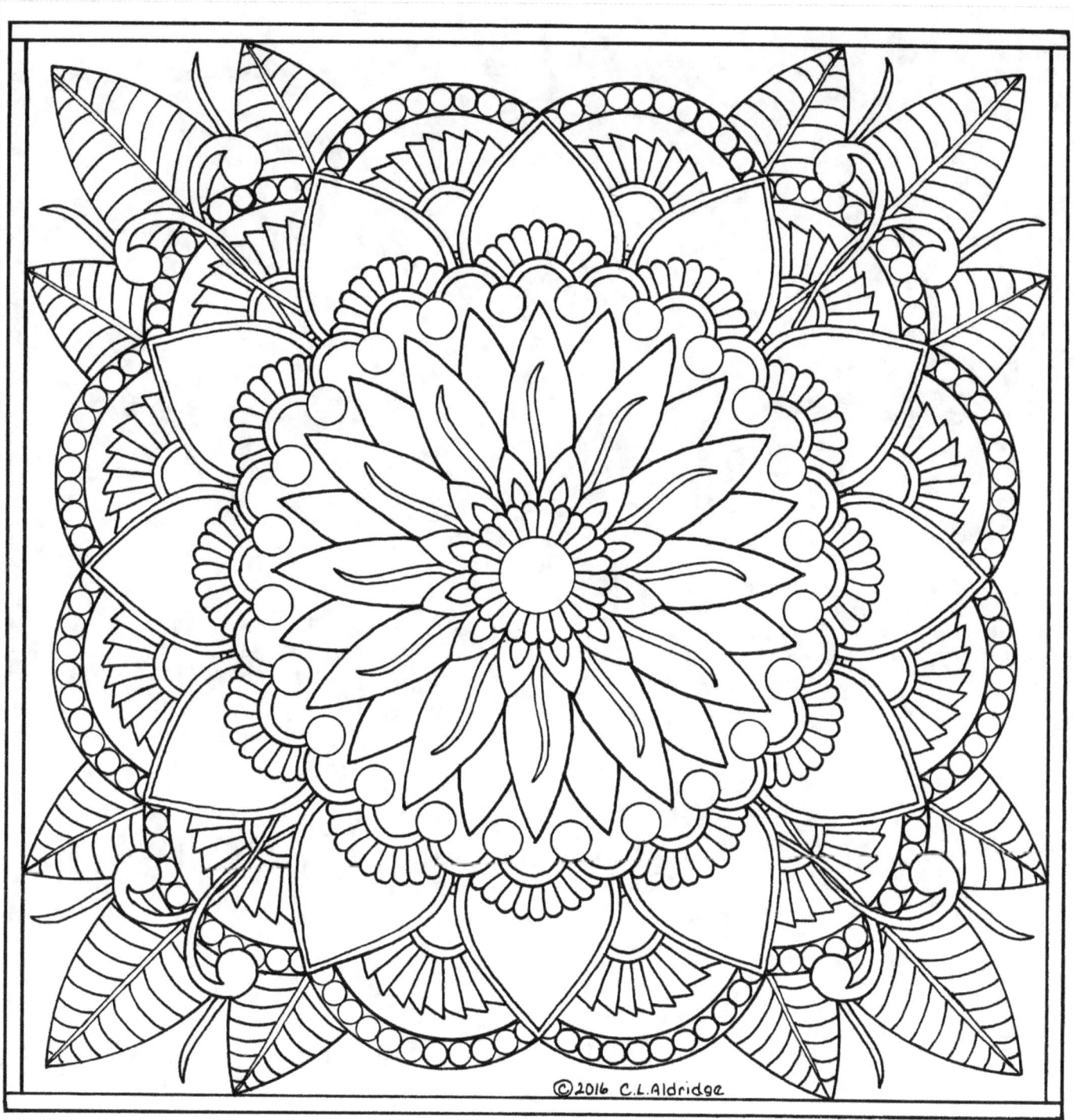

©2016 C.L.Aldridge

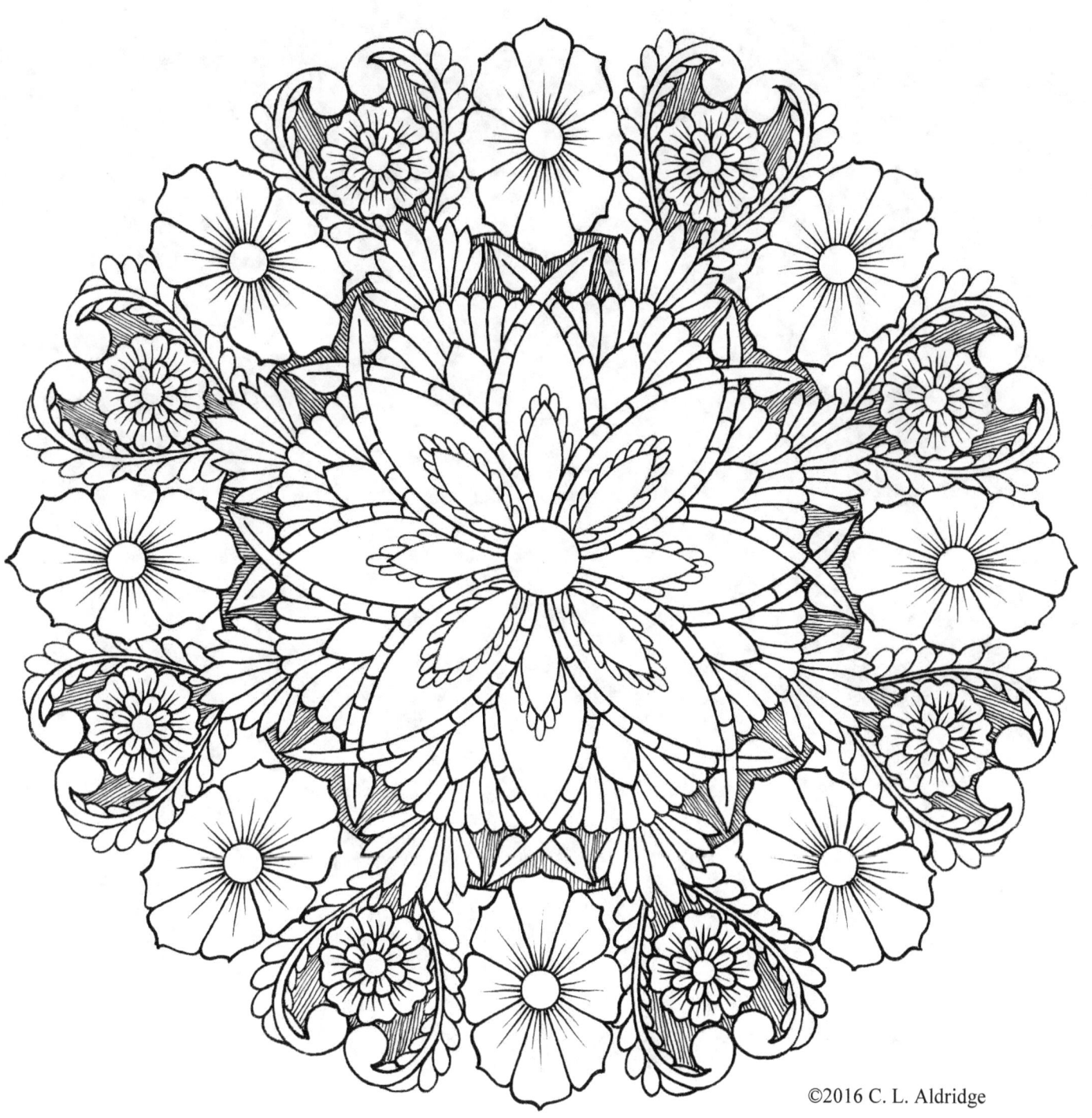

©2016 C. L. Aldridge

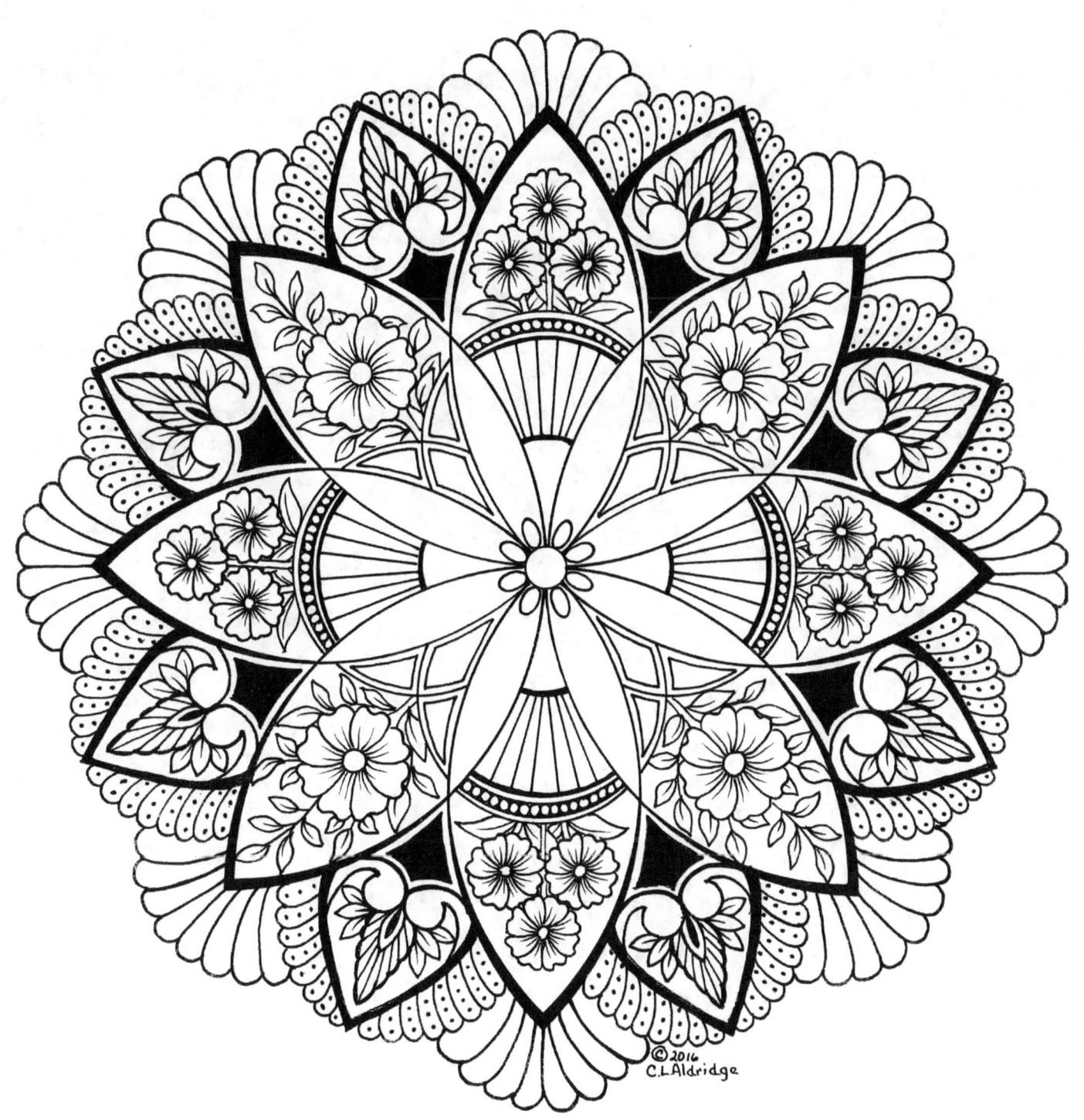

©2016
C.L.Aldridge

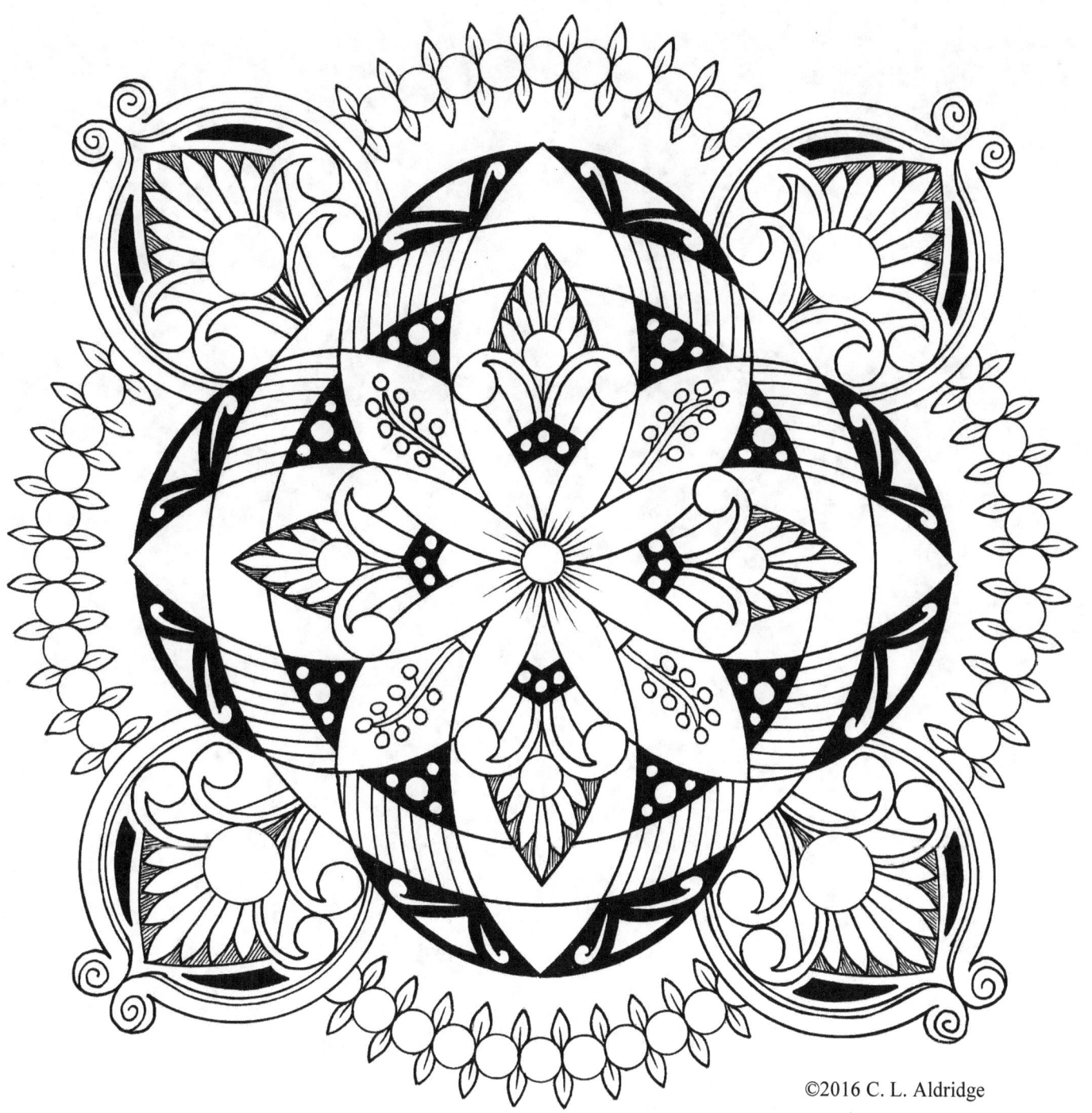

©2016 C. L. Aldridge

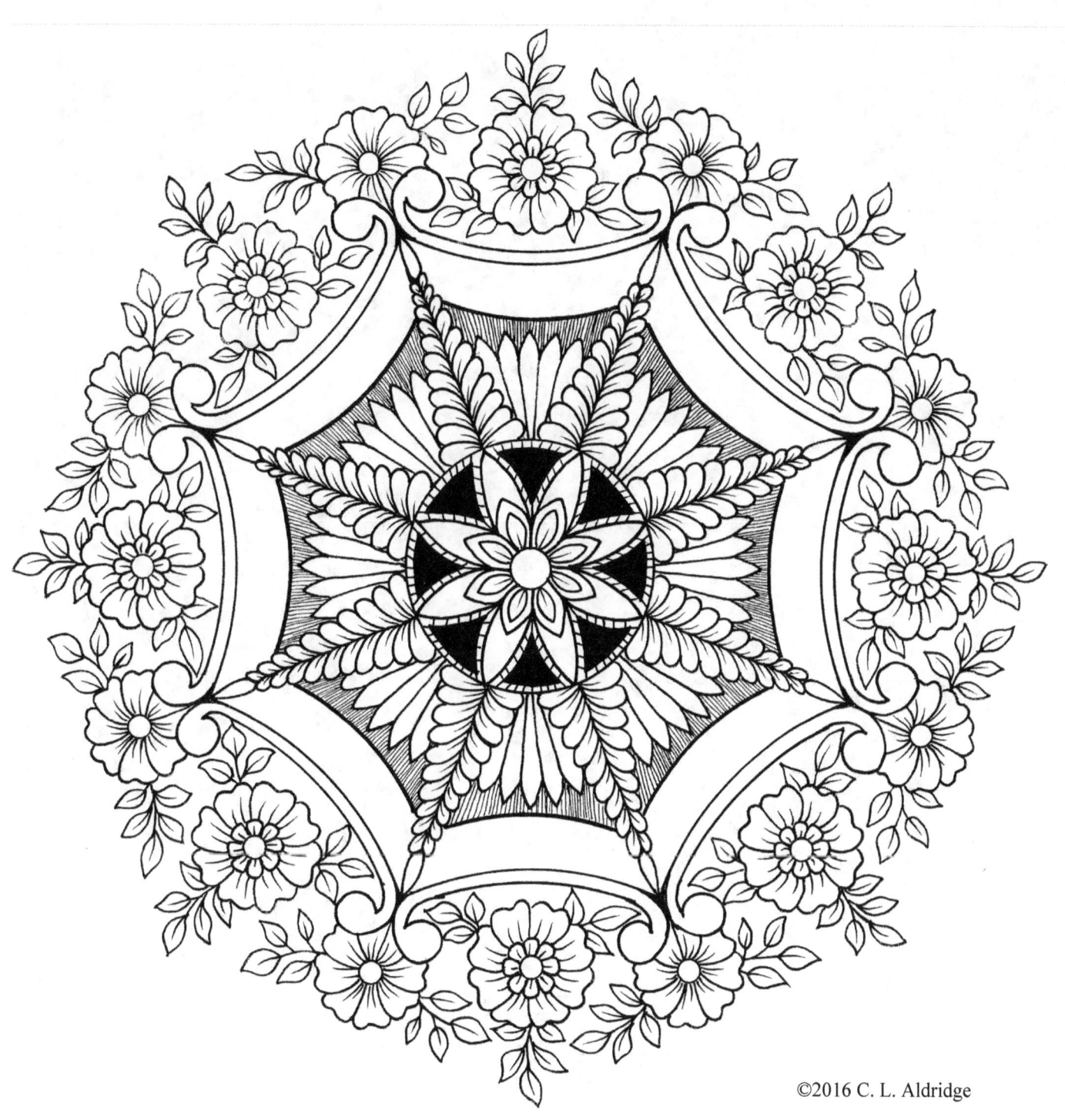

©2016 C. L. Aldridge

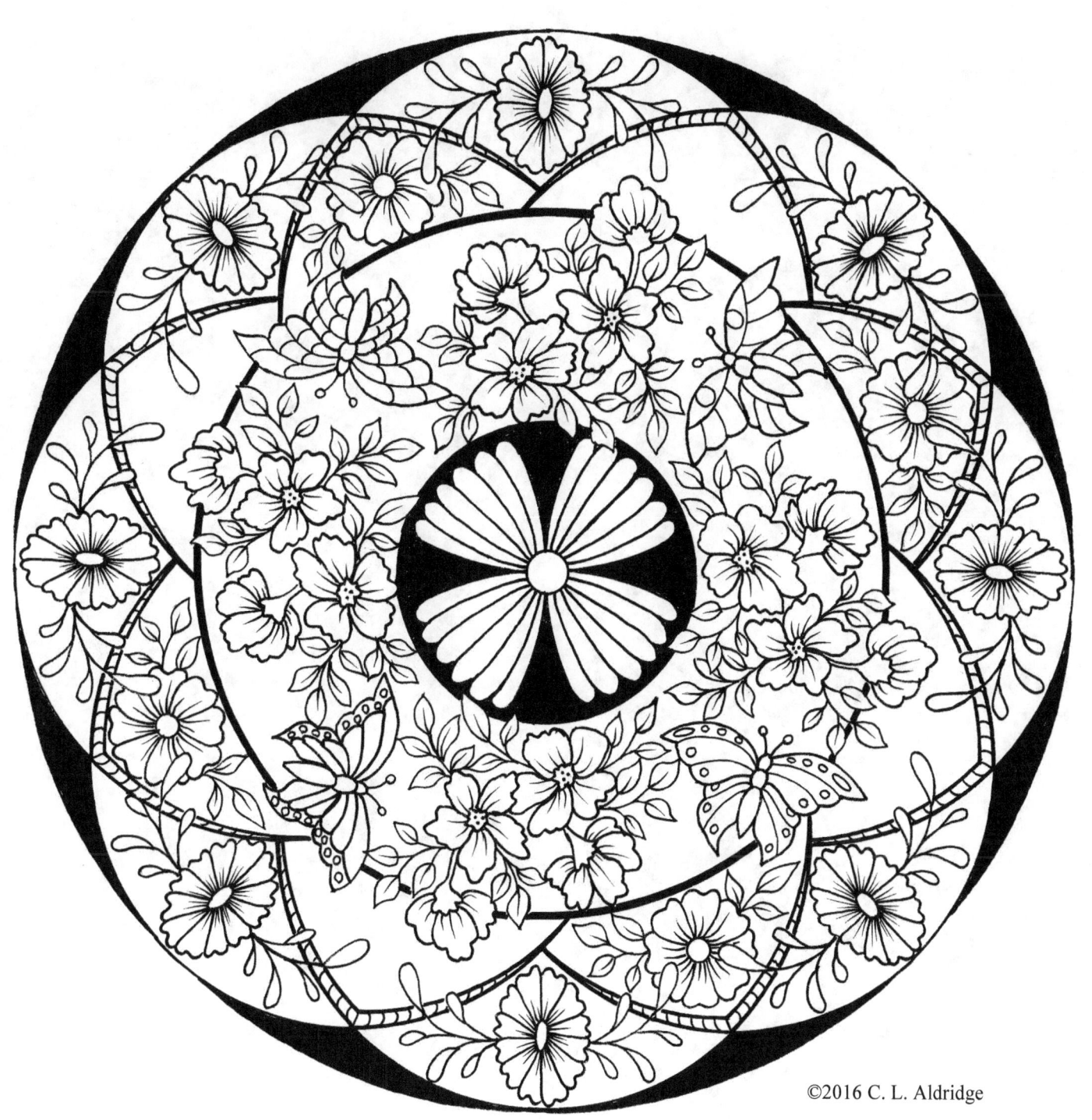

BONUS PAGES

12 adapted versions of the larger drawings, perfect for framing (5" x 7"), or for crafting, scrapbooking, and making greeting cards!

Also great for working out your color schemes for the larger drawings.

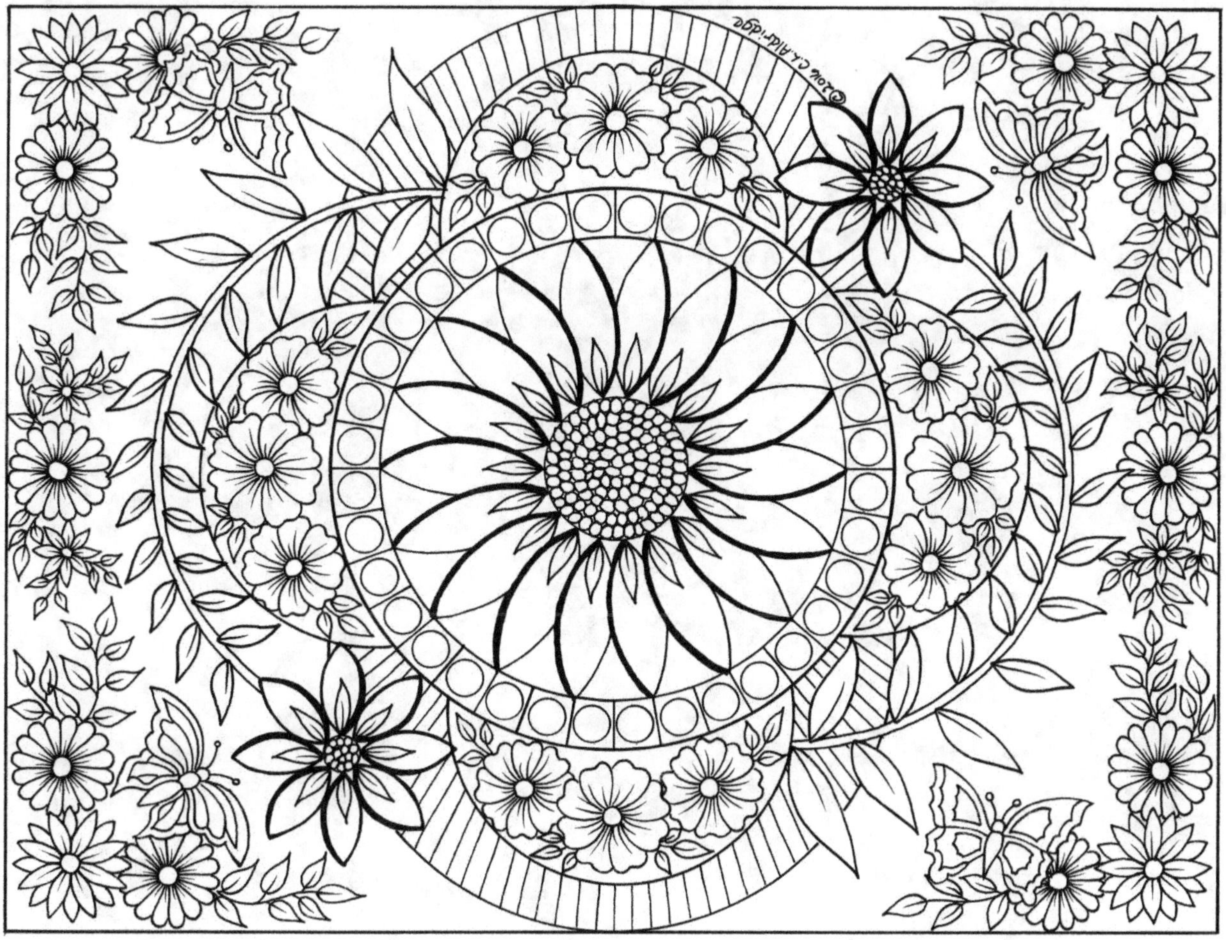
©2016 C.L.Aldridge

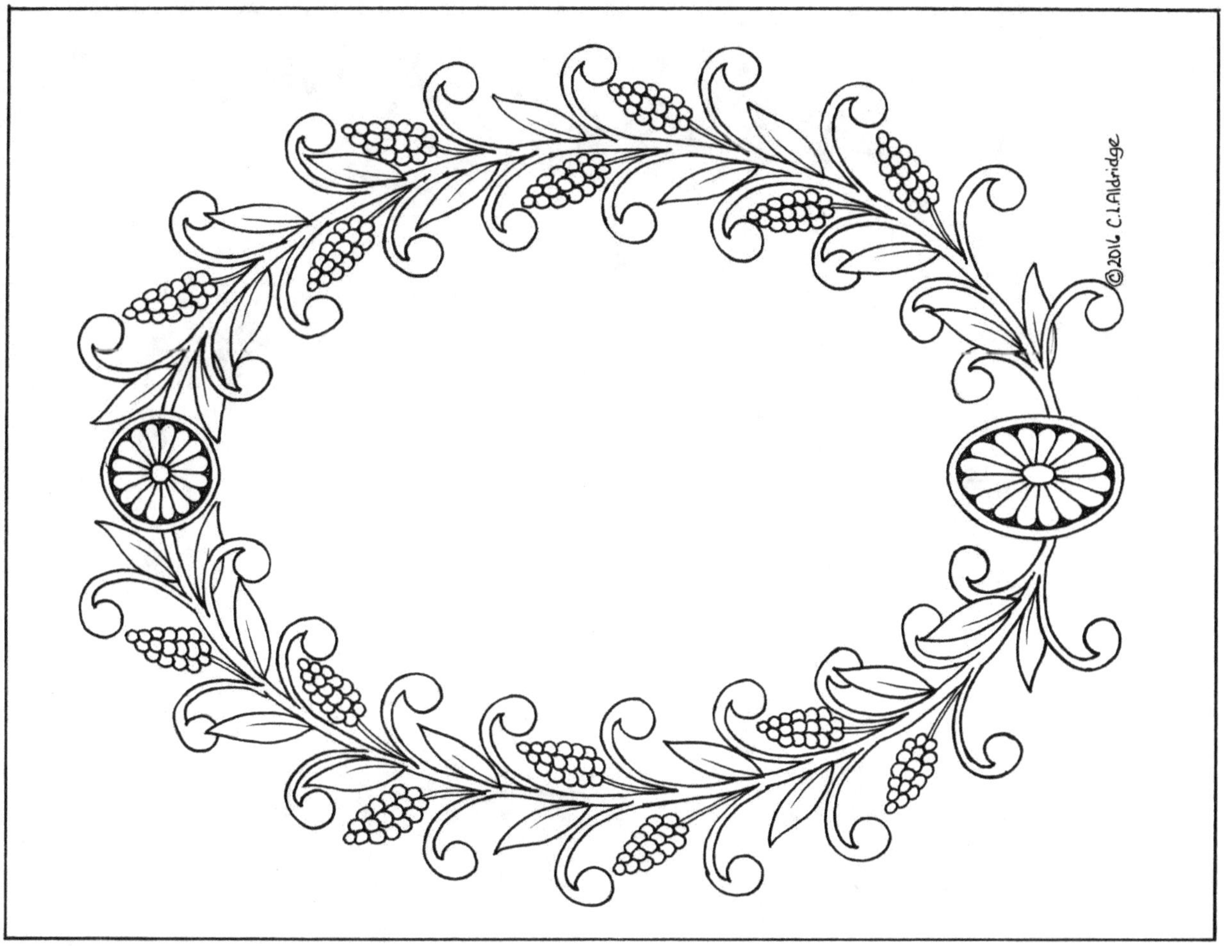
©2016 C.L.Aldridge

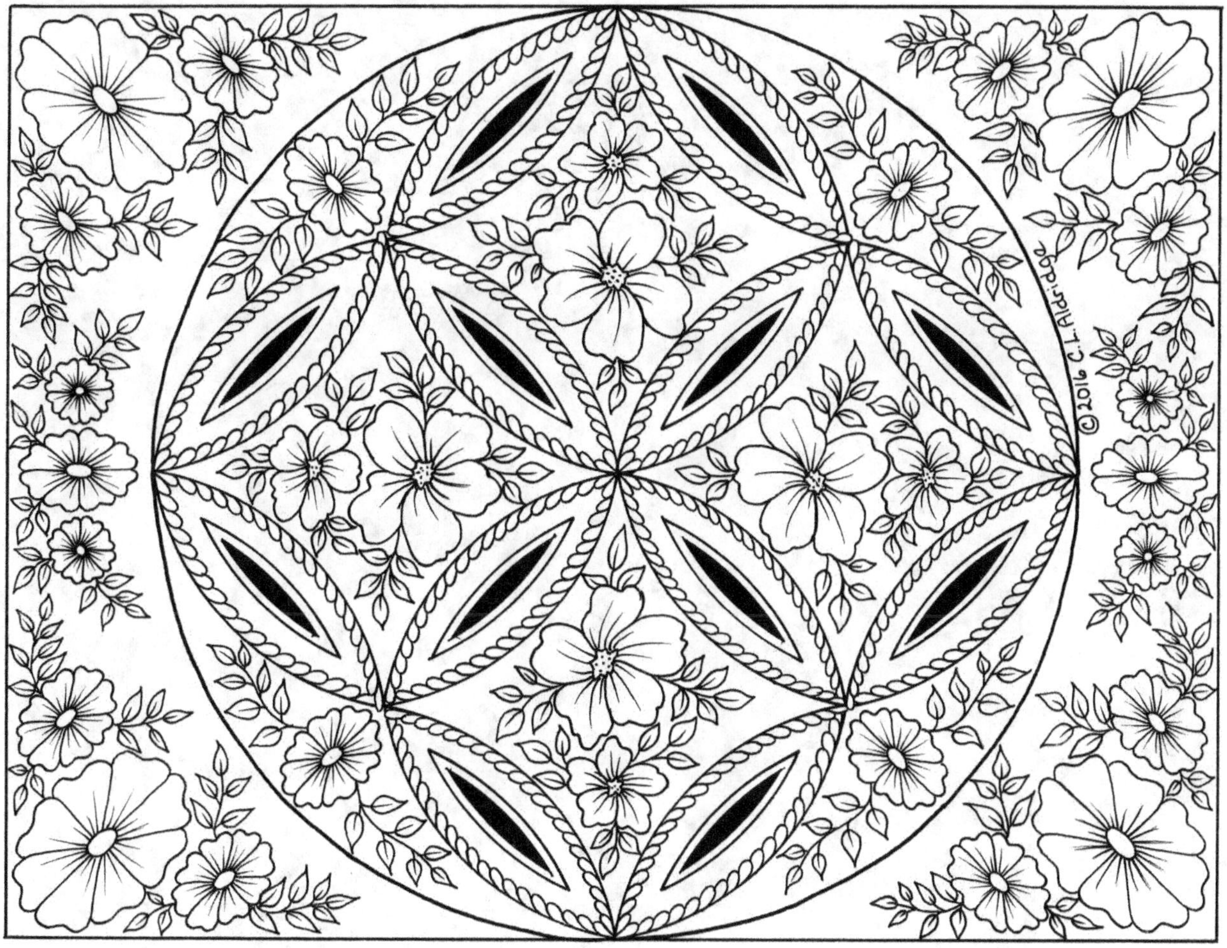

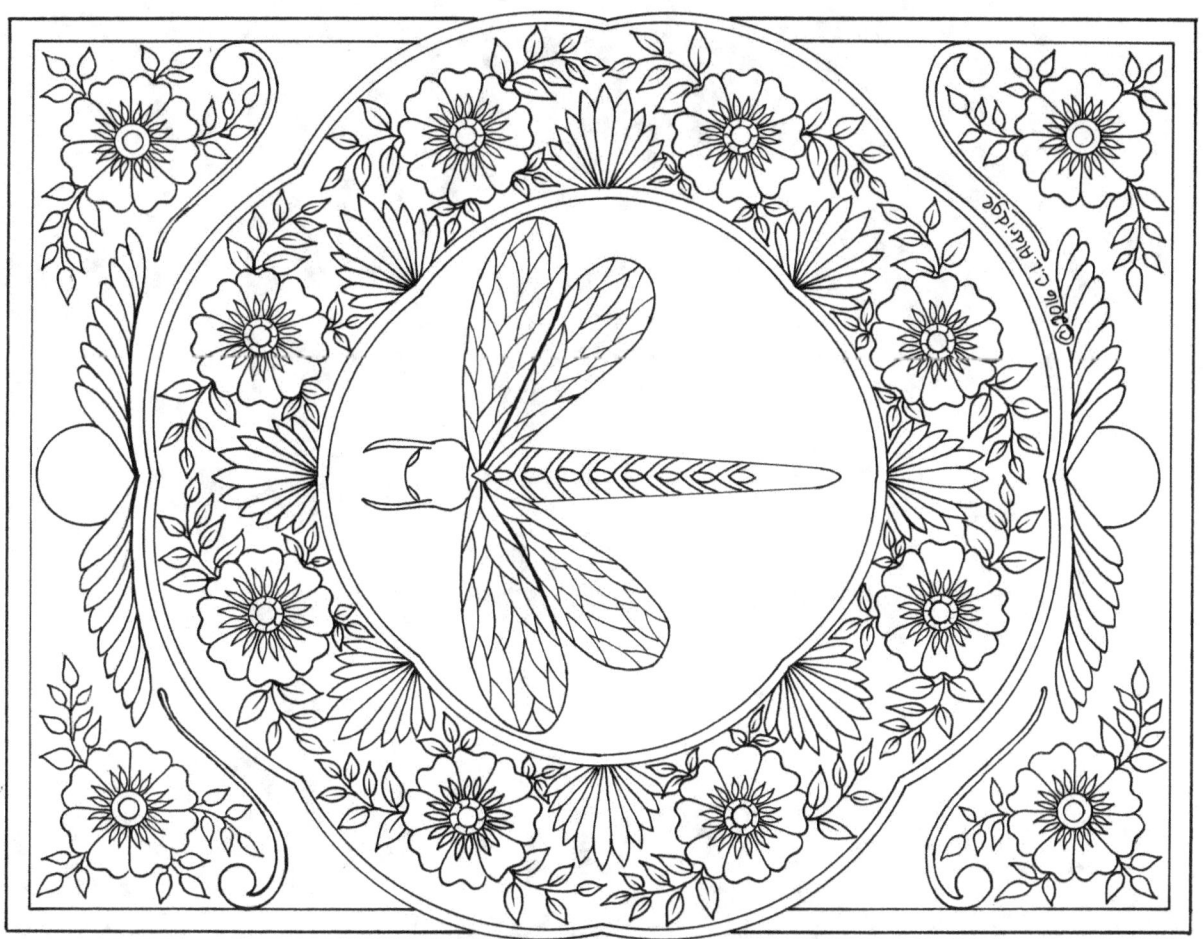

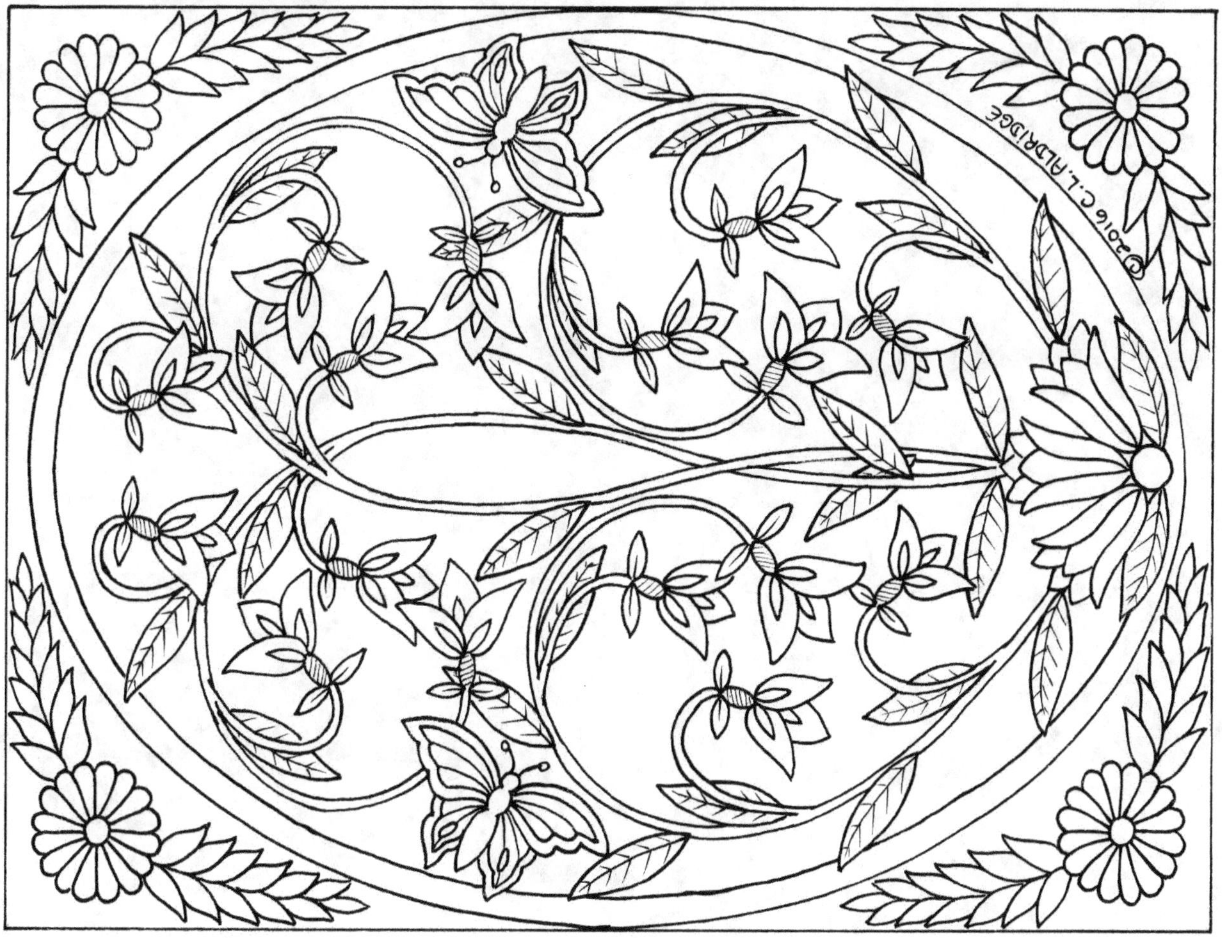
©2016 C.L.ALDRIDGE

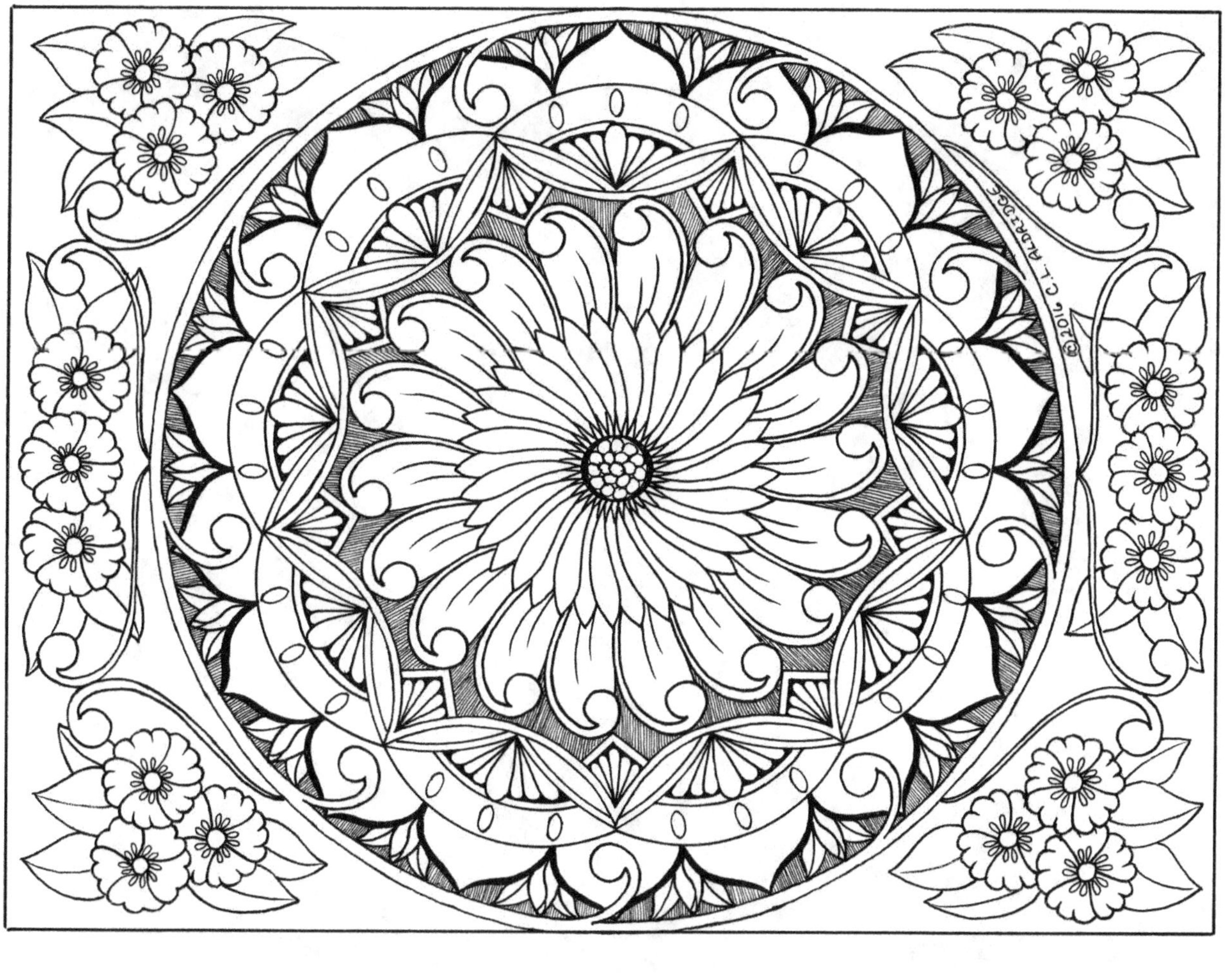
©2016 C.L.ALDRIDGE

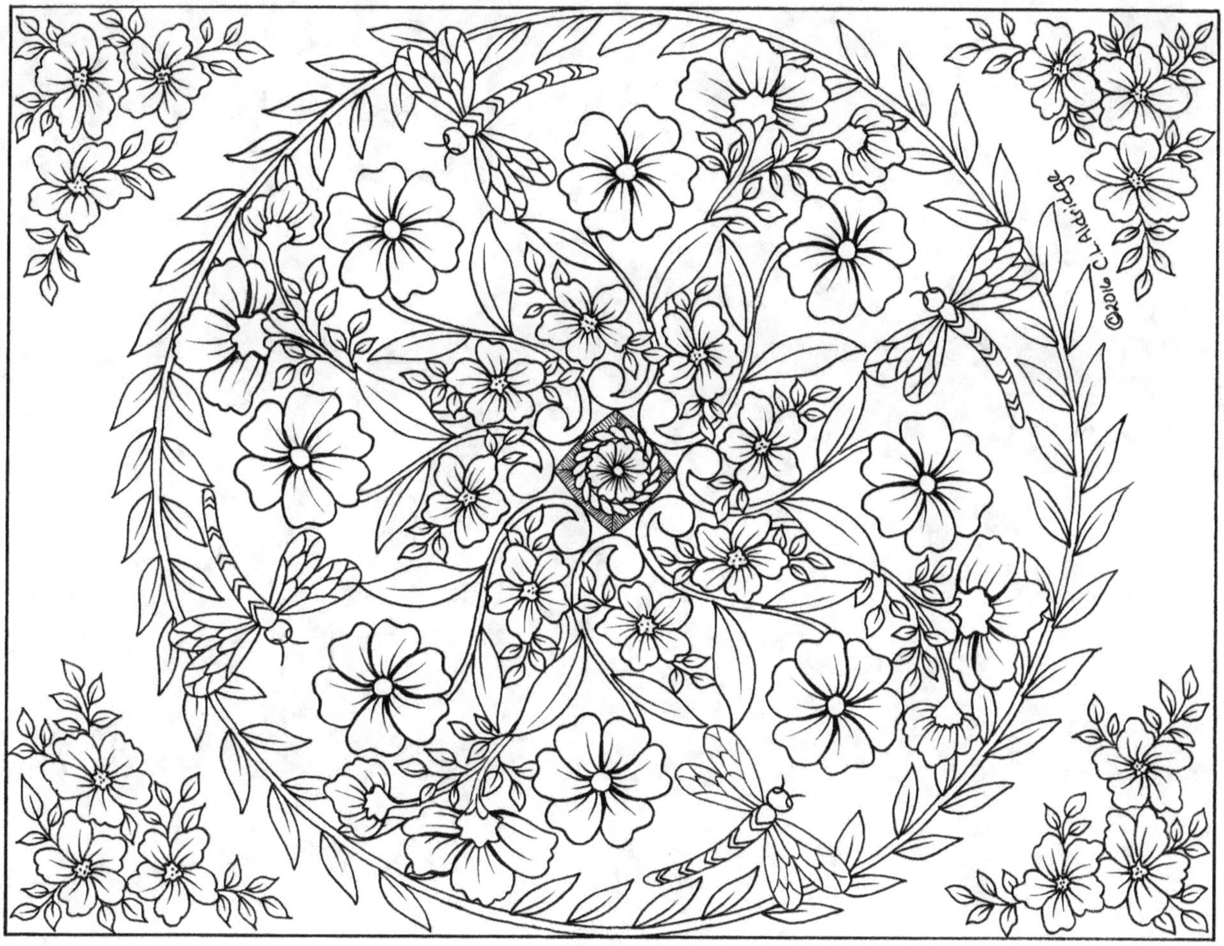

©2016 C.L. Aldridge

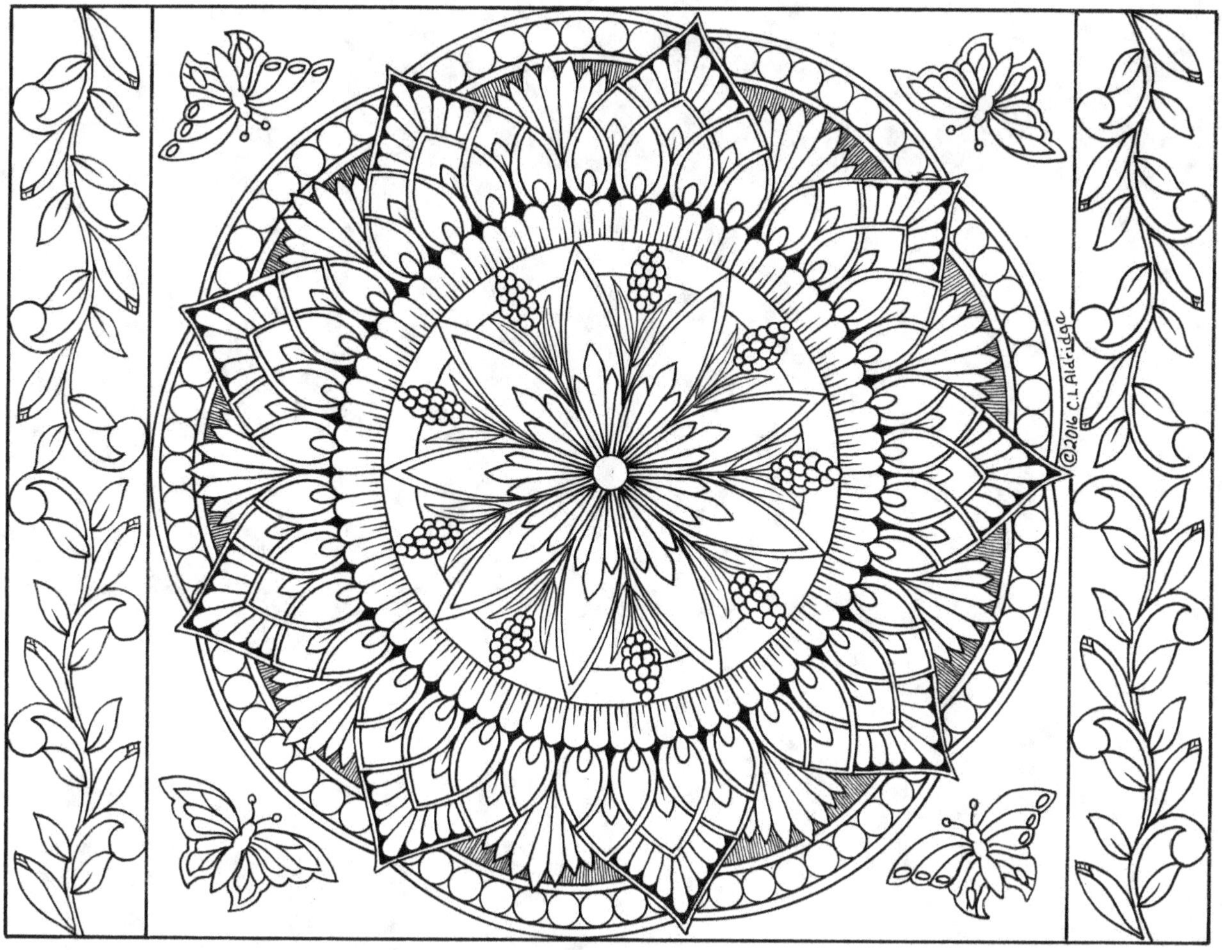

©2016 C.L. Aldridge

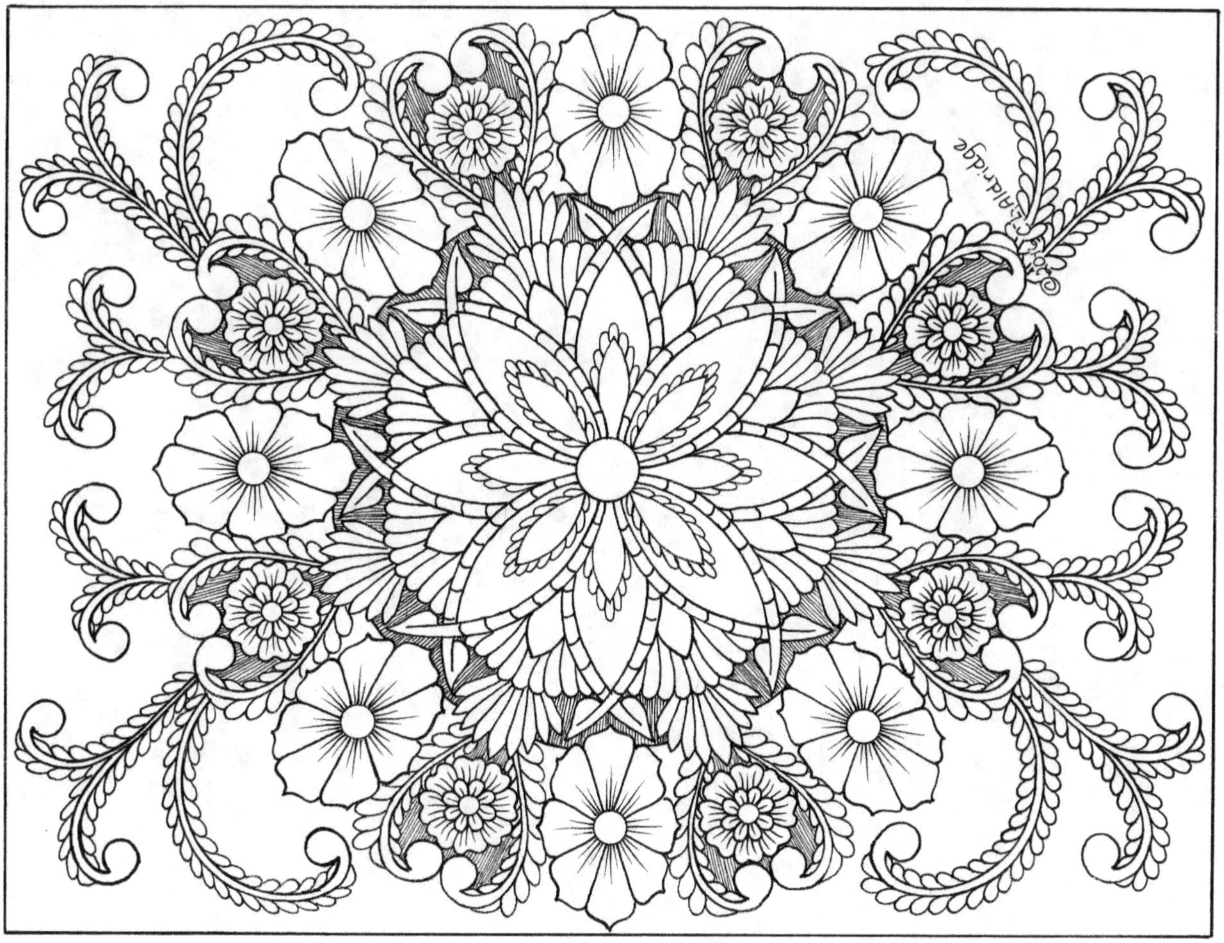

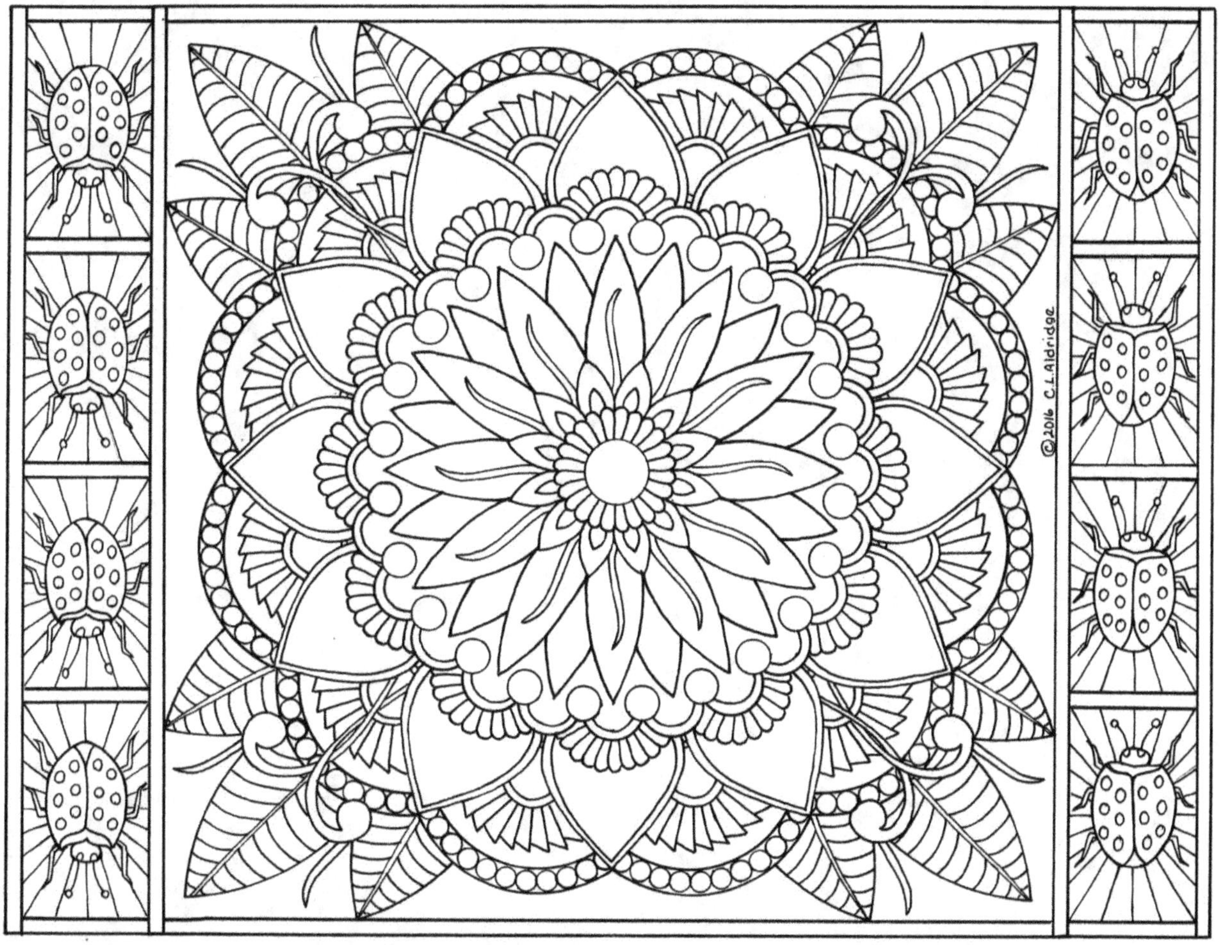
©2016 C.L.Aldridge

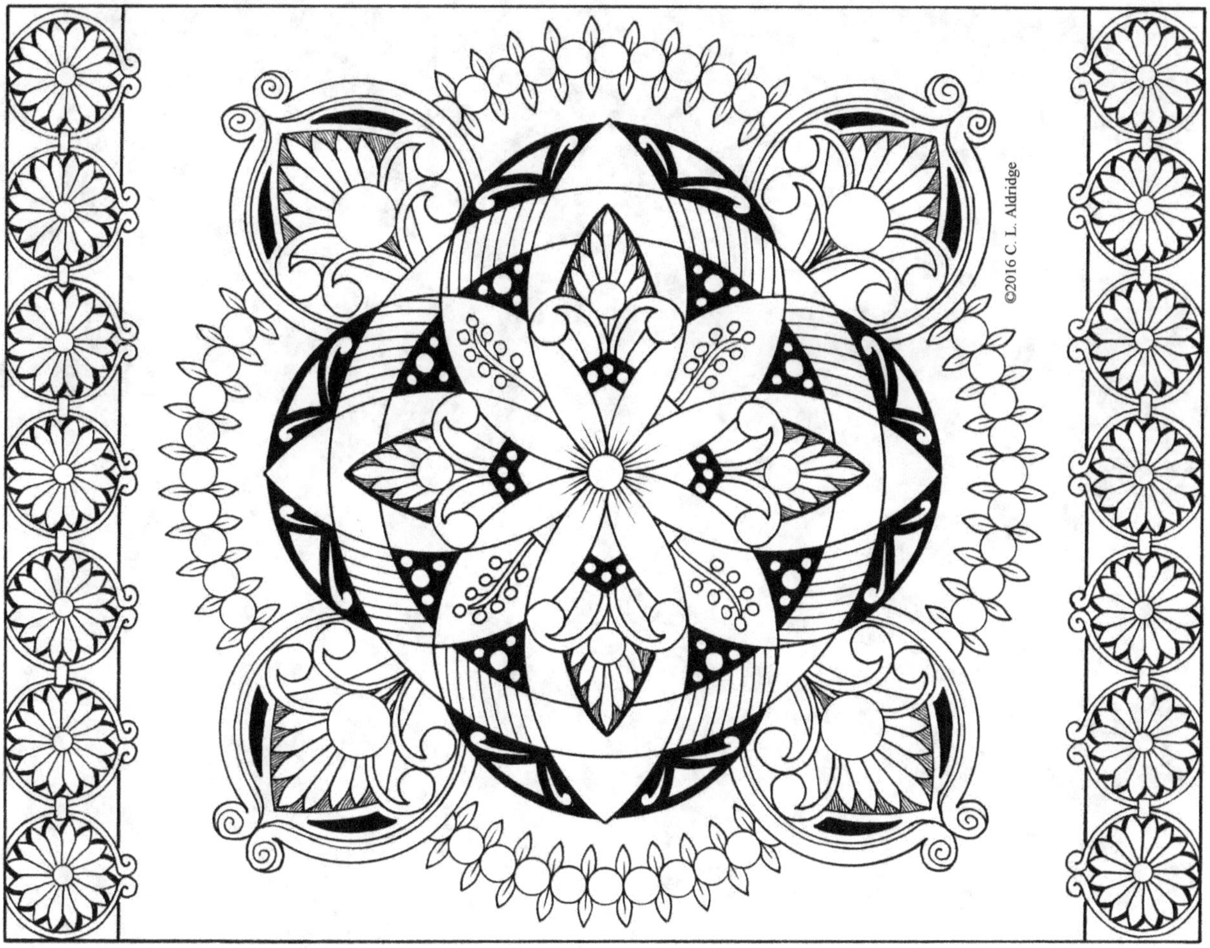
©2016 C. L. Aldridge

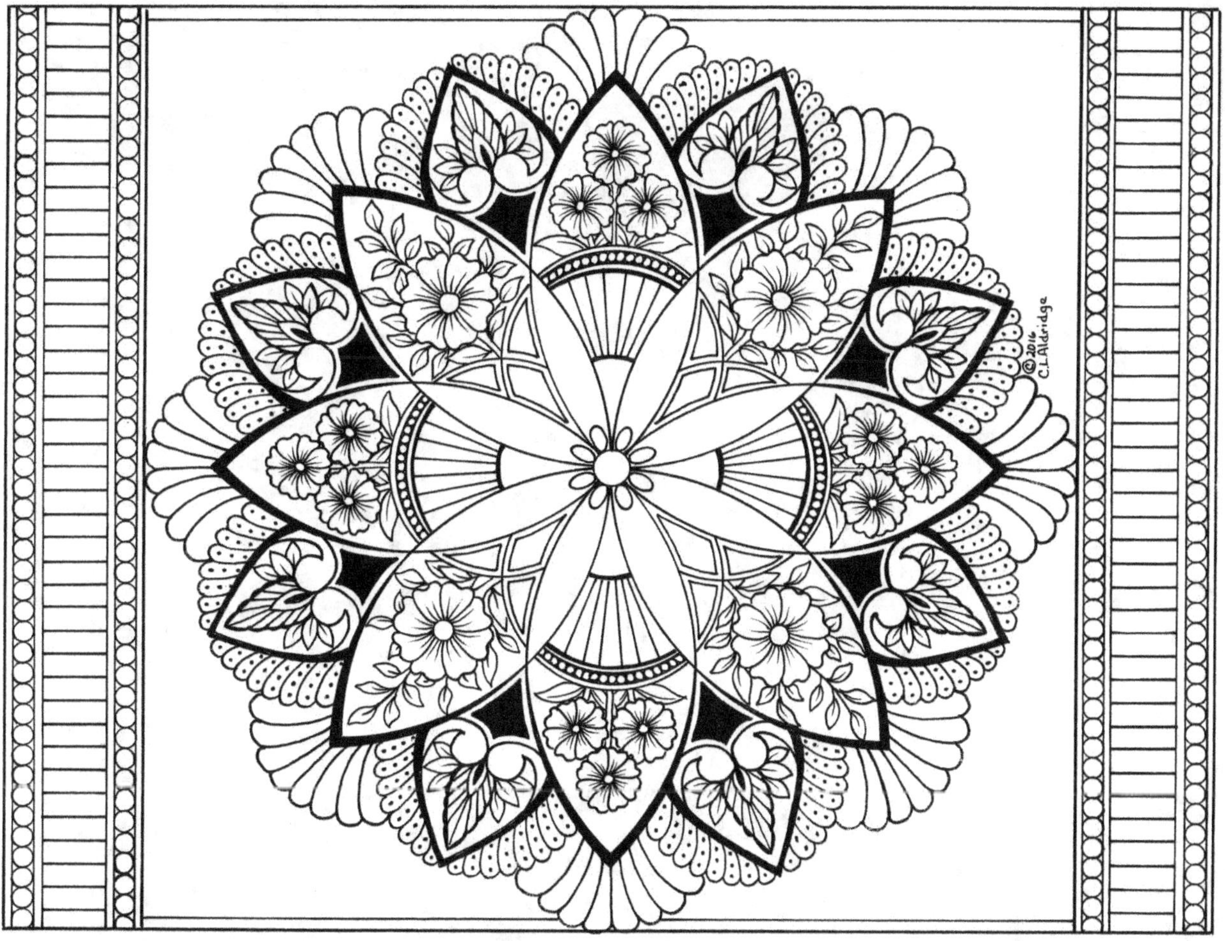
©2016 C.L.Aldridge

EVEN MORE BONUS PAGES!

Not long ago I had a fan who went treasure hunting in my picture archives and unearthed six drawings I had done long before I ever thought of creating coloring books for the print market. Though I argued that they were too ink heavy (lots of black ink), she encouraged me to at least offer them as PDF downloads from my Etsy shop at CLAldridgeArt. To my surprise they have been quite popular and have been beautifully colored and posted to Social Media several times.

Now I offer them to you to try out too!

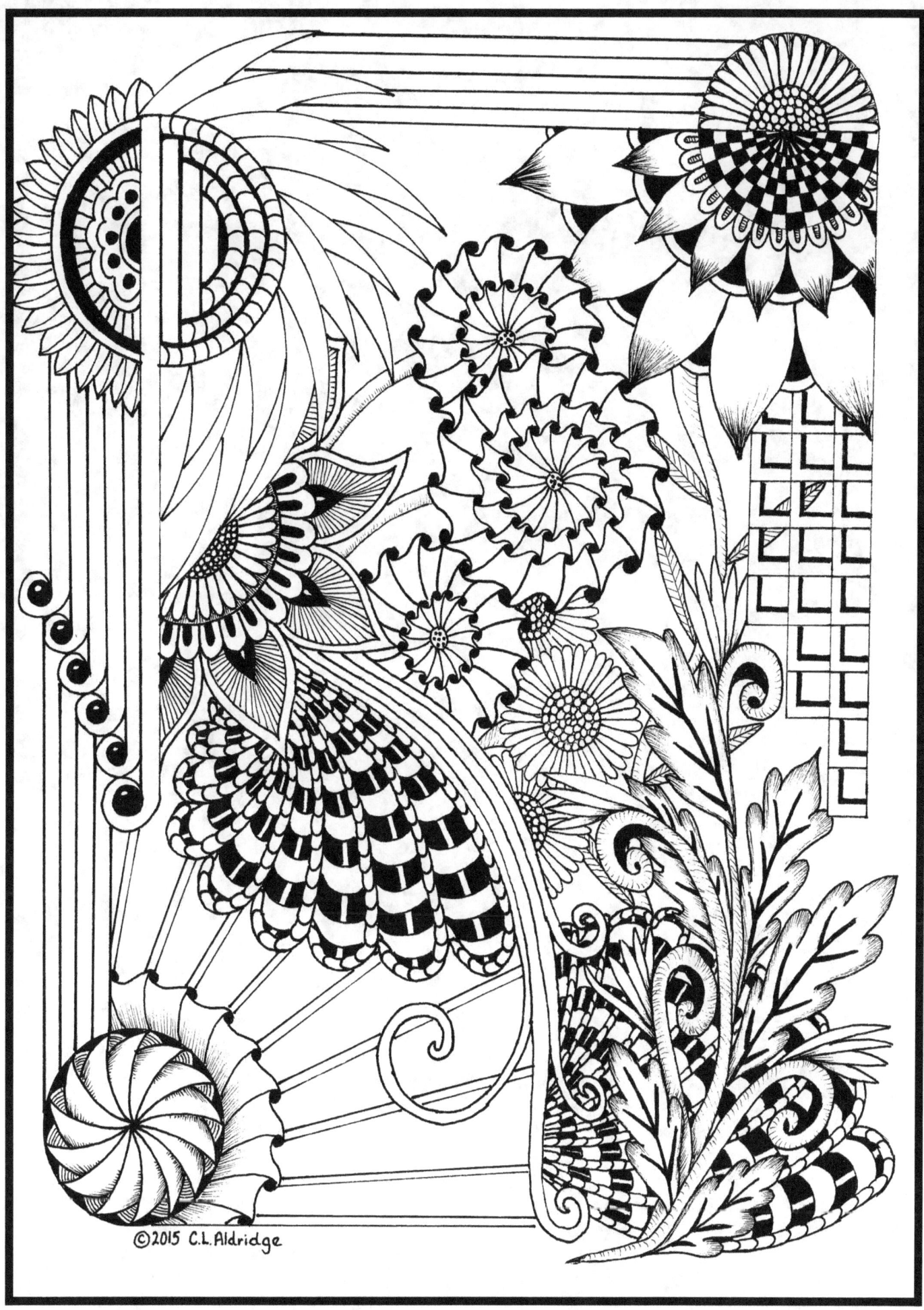

©2015 C.L. Aldridge

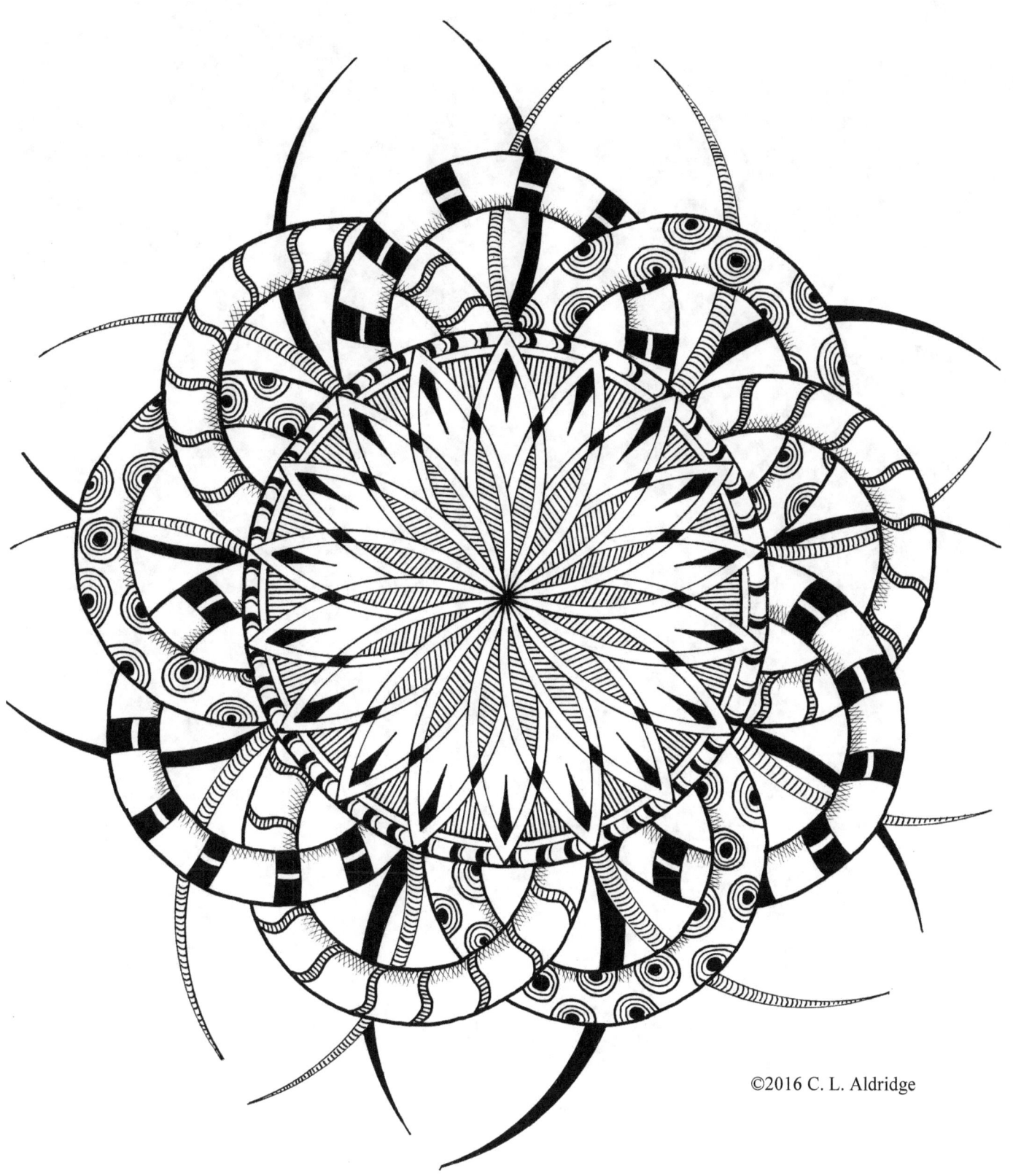

©2016 C. L. Aldridge

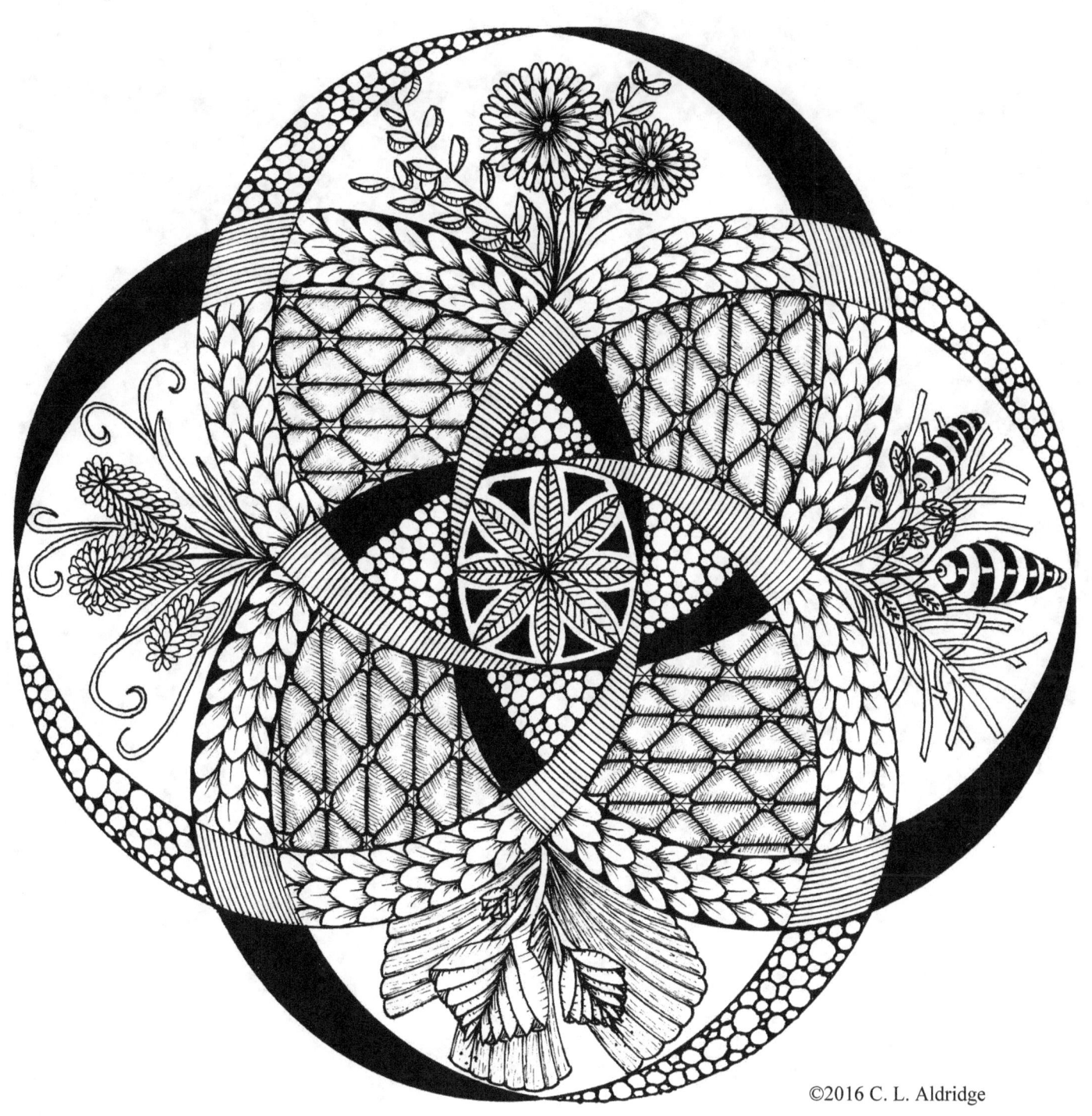

©2016 C. L. Aldridge

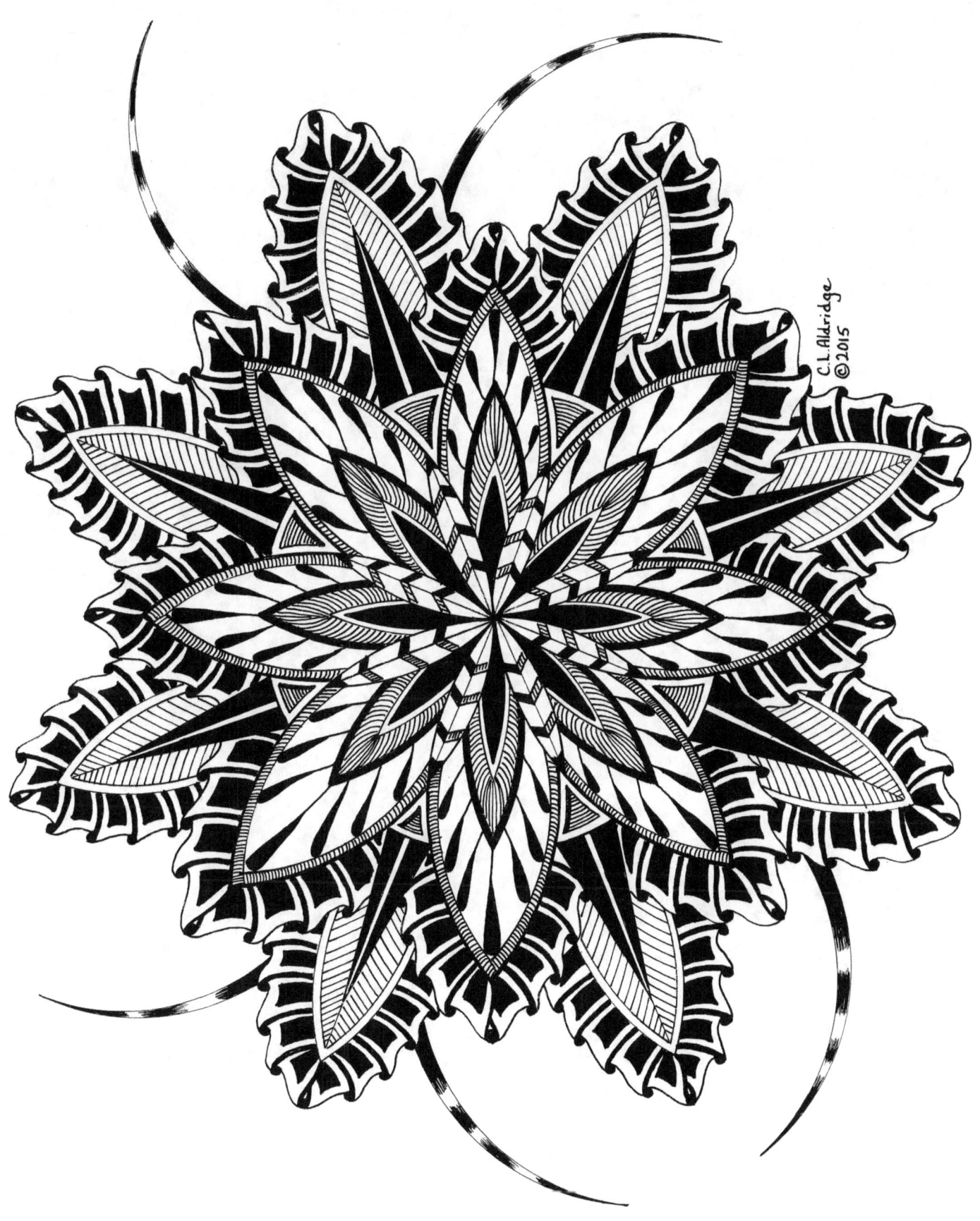

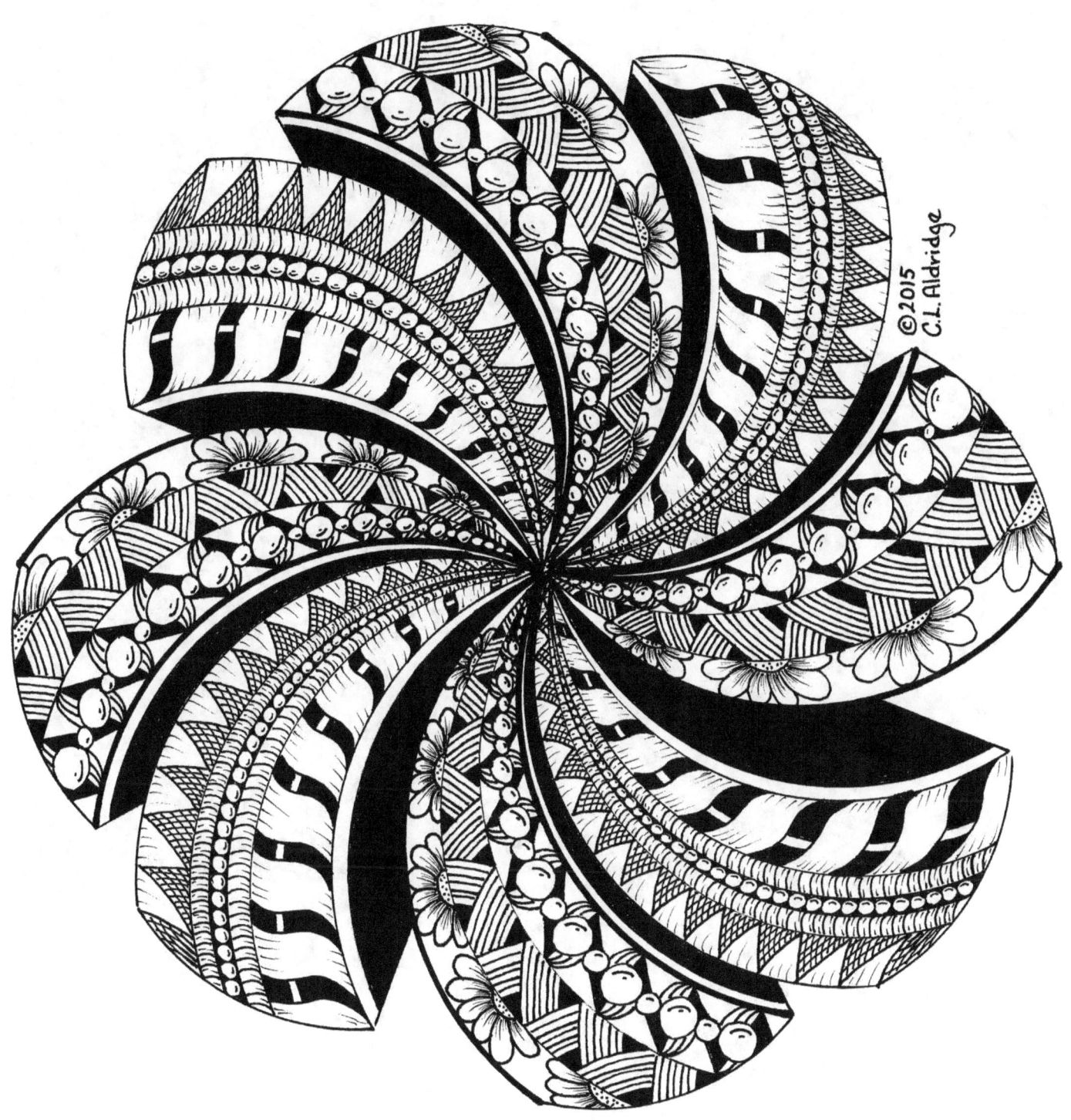

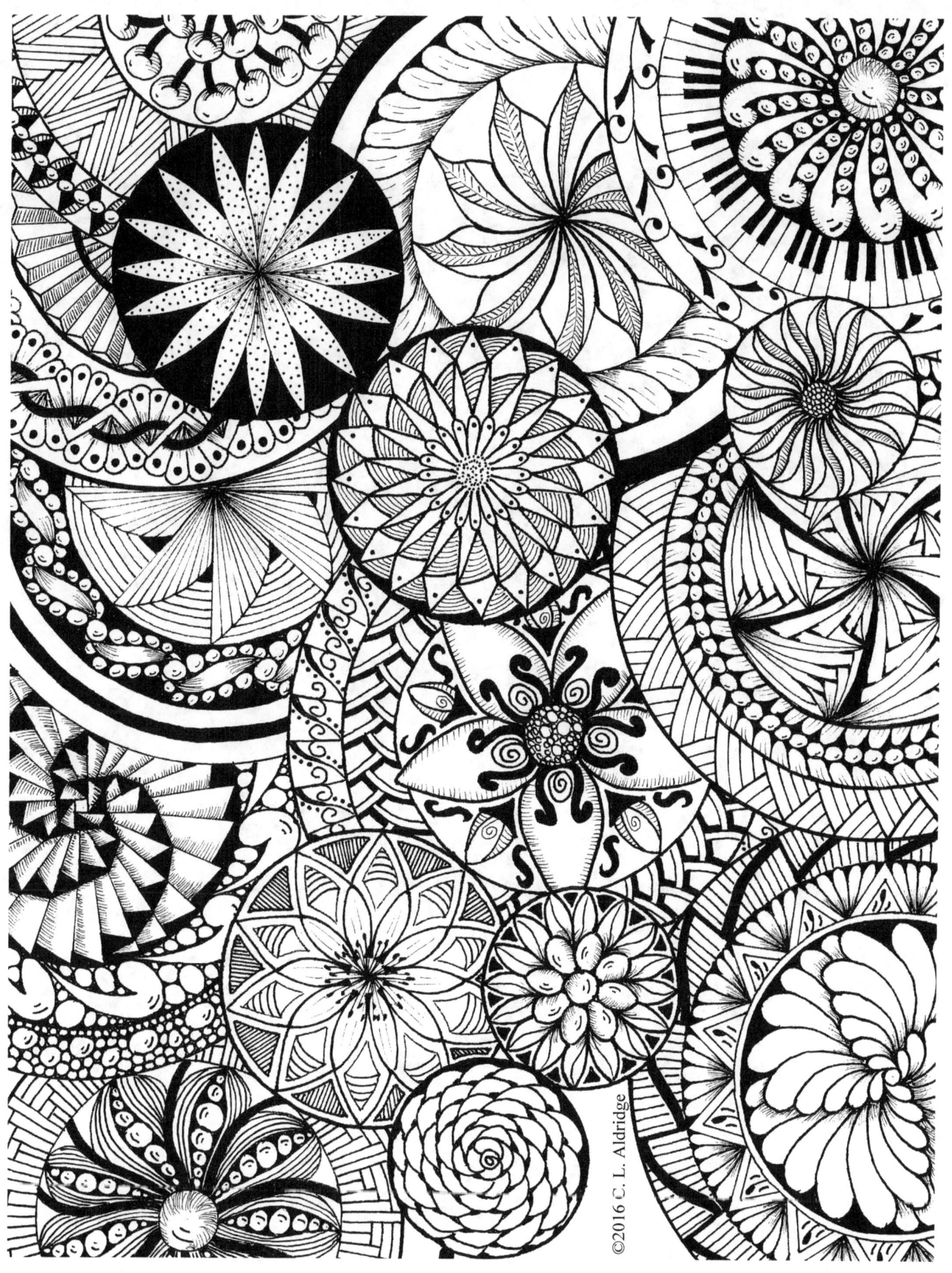

©2016 C. L. Aldridge

This page has intentionally been left blank for use as either
a blotting page or color testing page.

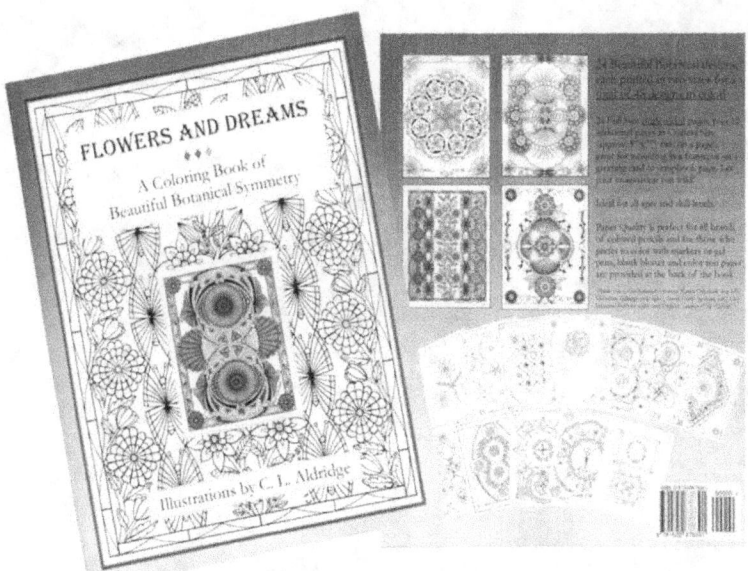

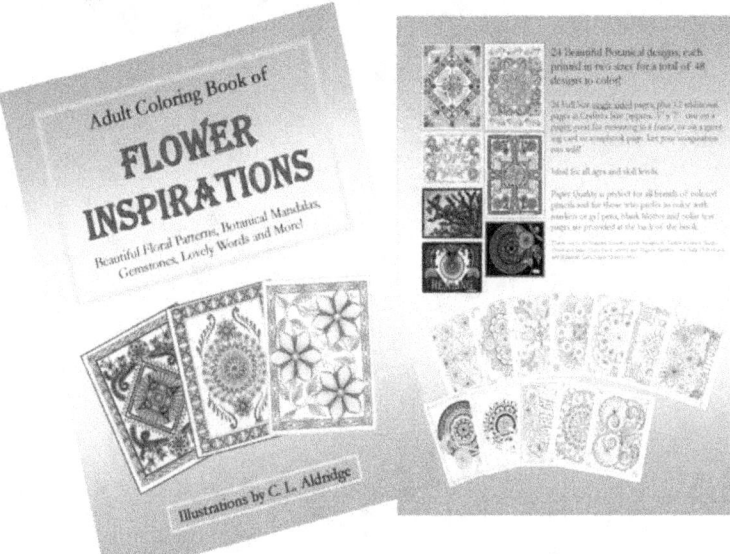

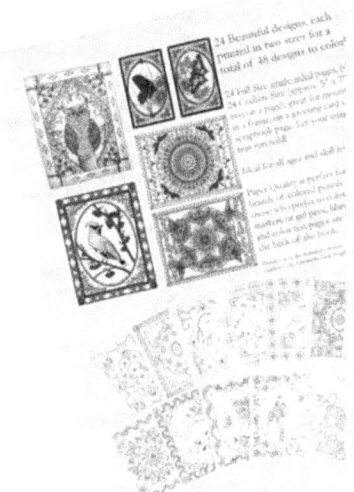

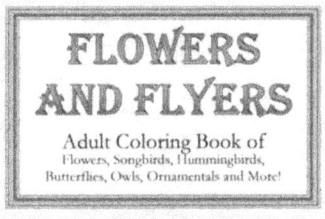

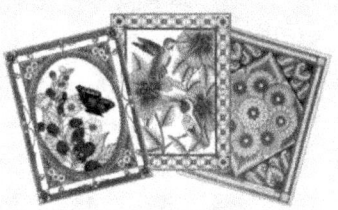

PUBLICATIONS/BODY OF WORK

FLOWERS AND DREAMS
A Coloring Book of Beautiful
Botanical Symmetry

**ADULT COLORING BOOK OF
FLOWER INSPIRATIONS**
Beautiful Floral Patterns, Botanical Mandalas
Gemstones, Lovely Words and More!

FLOWERS AND FLYERS
Adult Coloring Book of
Flowers, Songbirds, Hummingbirds,
Butterflies, Owls, Ornamentals and More!

**FLOWERS, BIRDS, BUTTERFLIES
AND MORE!**, Travel Size Book of:
Your Coloring Book for the Road

Www. ETSY.com/CLALDRIDGEART
PDF versions of Books
and Individual Pages

Collaborations

ADULT COLORING BOOK TREASURY
110 Illustrations from 55 Artists

ADULT COLORING BOOK TREASURY 2
130 Illustrations from 70 Artists

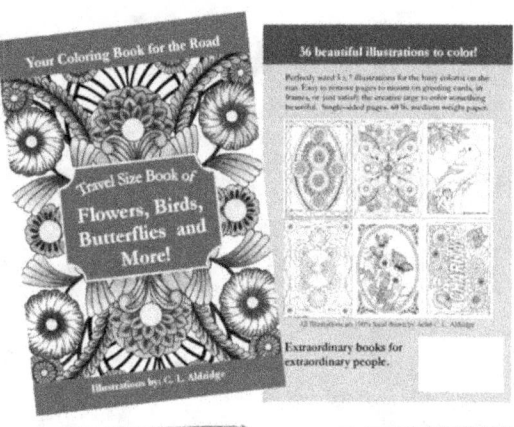